Stronger on the Other Side

The Power to Choose

Andrea Heuston

First printing, 2021.

Lead Like a Woman Press
371 NE Gilman Blvd
Suite 245
Issaquah, Washington 98027

www.strongerontheotherside.net

ISBN: 978-1-7923-6533-1

Praise for Stronger on the Other Side

"Andrea's story will change the way you think about your own power of choice. I was sucked into Andrea's vivid, funny, and honest stories about what it means to choose happiness, use your voice, and stand in your power. *Stronger on the Other Side* opens up space and possibility to explore your own beliefs around living a life filled with more joy and more love."
– Danielle Johnson, Founder and CEO, Cannon
 Leadership Group

"More than memoir, this book has actionable steps at the end of each chapter to help us on our path to being *Stronger on the Other Side*. The issues of control, of searching for what we want and need, of being "other" when we want so desperately to fit in resonated deeply with me. I read it in one sitting, with tears in my eyes and recognition in my heart."
– Andrea Herrera, Founder & President, Amazing
 Edibles & Boxperience

"The purpose of *Stronger on the Other Side* is to model resilience and success through hardship, and joy through struggle. Andrea provides a roadmap for all badass women who know there is more out there than the world often shows. What a gift to call her friend."
– Amanda Skey, Kindergarten Teacher

"*Strong on the Other Side: The Power to Choose*, follows Andrea Heuston's journey – from a quiet and subservient girl to a stronger woman who now lives 'on the other side.' She will show you all the deep, complex trials she experienced as a roadmap to a much different place. These are invaluable lessons for all of us."
– Hao Lam, CEO of Best in Class Education,
  Author of *From Bad to Worse to Best in Class*

"Andrea Heuston captures real-life lessons to help propel you further and faster on your own journey. Learn vicariously as Andrea masterfully shares her experiences with honesty and candor."
– Fran Biderman-Gross, Co-Author of the bestselling book, *How to Lead a Values-Based Professional Services Firm*

For Eric, Aidan, and Owen.
You are my heart.

Disclaimer

Dear Reader,

If you are offended by swear words, such as shit or fuck, you may want to stop reading this book now. Sometimes I lack a better word choice that encapsulates my feelings.

Table of Contents

Foreword 11

Introduction..15

Section 1: Other 31

    The Other Side of Other 32

    Some Version of Other..34

    Other Shit..37

    Women are Other at Birth 39

    My Version of Other 42

    I Goofed. Again. 45

    Cookie Dough and Judgment 49

    The Nerd 51

    Confusing Dichotomies 54

    Getting Through the Unhappy..................................56

    I Figured it Out..59

    Wow, I Can Do This 61

    Denmark 63

    Home...66

    Adulting...68

    Oh Shit, I Othered Myself..72

    Stronger on the Other Side of Other 75

    Practice...77

Section 2: Broken...79

The Other Side of Broken................................80

The Broken Side of Broken 81

But I Could Control it, Right?.........................83

Once a Month Death 85

Old Eggs...87

Gambling on One Round................................89

We Got Nothing..91

Dark and Powerless..93

Adoption 96

S, the Birth Mother 99

Aidan...101

Hi. Do You Want Another Baby?..................104

Owen 107

Family of Choice...109

We Got Everything..114

From Mom to Mother....................................115

Stronger on the Other Side of Broken...........117

Practice 119

Section 3: Unconscious 121

The Other Side of Unconscious 122

I Was Fat...124

Something's Wrong..128

June 2008 130

Truly Unconscious...132

I Woke Up 136

Home 139

Recovery...142

Owning It..144

Stronger on the Other Side of Unconscious...........146

Conscious at Home 148

Conscious at Work 151

Conscious in Life 153

Practice...155

Section 4: Fire 157

The Other Side of Fire............................158

My Relationship with Fire 159

August 4th, 2014 162

The Aftermath 168

Controlling the Narrative 173

Cataloging the House 175

Rebuilding..177

I Missed My House 179

Stronger on the Other Side of Fire 182

Practice...185

Section 5: It's Okay to be Sad 187

The Other Side of Grief...........................188

Grief from Death 190

Joy from Grief...192

Hope from Grief......................................195

Guardian Angels from Grief 197

Learning from Grief 200

Stronger on the Other Side of Grief 205

Practice 209

Final Thoughts 211
    Stronger on the Other Side 212
    We Are Enough 214

Acknowledgements 217

Foreword

Congratulations on having the amazing good sense to pick up *Stronger on the Other Side* by my friend and colleague Andrea Heuston. Andrea has been walking around with this book in her head for a long time, and I'm so delighted that she is finally sharing her story. *Stronger on the Other Side* is a journey into a life that is both unremarkably normal and kind of freakish. I mean, my friend has lived some shit that will take your breath away.

I first met Andrea at an event hosted by Entrepreneur's Organization (EO), a professional organization we both belong to, in Hawaii. At the time, I was dealing with some of my own shit and showed up at the Regional Leadership Academy event feeling like I wanted to hide, emotionally and physically beat down, and trying not to show it. Anyone who knows me well may be surprised that I ever feel that way (or would even admit it). Andrea—being the insightful leader she is—saw through my bravado, and we formed a strong, instant bond based on personal and professional sisterhood. I am now forever blessed with long girlfriend conversations into the night, monthly meetings, and the wisdom that she gives to me.

And now you, too, can have the gift that is Andrea through this book. You will laugh, gasp, cry, cheer, and want to be her friend (but get in line, bitches!). She is a fierce fighter for women who has been knocked on her ass multiple times—seriously, you won't believe the stories—and keeps getting back up.

Andrea has written *Stronger on the Other Side* so that you can use her life circumstances to inform your own. This book will support you in examining and choosing perhaps a new angle on perception and reflection of your typical ways of reacting and responding to life. After reading her story, you'll certainly relate to your own shit in a different way. I know I do!

I encourage you to spend some thought and time on the exercises at the end of each chapter—they're worth your precious time.

My favorite quote from Andrea is this: "Don't apologize for who you are. Your path is your own and no one else's." You'll feel that in your bones by the time you reach the final pages of her book.

Andrea has honored me twice, first by inviting me to be the debut guest on her *Lead Like a Woman* podcast (go back and check out the first episode) and now by asking me to write the foreword for her book.

It is my dearest wish that you'll allow Andrea's words and experiences to bring power to your life! Enjoy the journey that is *Stronger on the Other Side!*

Dr. Kristin L. Kahle

Best-selling author of

Notivation: How to Use the Power of NO to Make Your First Million Dollars

Introduction

"Loving ourselves through the process of owning our story is the bravest thing we'll ever do." – Brené Brown

August 4, 2014, was a blissfully normal day at our beach house on the Washington coast. Until the fog—so heavy and cold that night—rolled in. Until the fire started. Until I, in pajamas and flip-flops, hugging my boys Aidan and Owen, stood in a neighbor's driveway and watched my beloved house begin to disappear as the fire, so bright against the night sky, ate it away.

I had given that house mystical powers. It was my happy place, the only place in the world I believed I could be my full authentic self, where I felt loved unconditionally, unjudged by the sea and the sand and the dune grasses that waved effortlessly between us and the water.

The fire that raged that night took my house, and me with it. For months after, I was pulled under, like part of me had been taken away. The thing I liked most about myself was gone. I struggled through many deep dark nights, for a long time, to get to the other side of that loss.

Eventually, I realized my bottomless grief was never about losing the house. I understood that the story I'd told myself about its magical love for me was pure bullshit. The truth is that I hadn't really lost anything that night. In fact, I'd found something. I'd been given a gift, really. And it was terrifying.

Something Lost. Something Found.

A round midnight, after the boys and I had stood shivering and watching the fire for nearly two hours, I sat in the back of a police vehicle and said to a friend over the phone, "I feel like every time I lose some humility, the universe knocks me on my ass with a lesson. This is a lesson I need to learn somehow."

I had no idea in the moment how prophetic my words would turn out to be—and mind you, this realization is coming from a woman who is no stranger to being knocked on her ass. After all, I'd had much experience previous to the fire that might have taught me what I eventually learned from it, including: I'm a female born in 1971, an era of conditioned sexism, misogyny, and 'other'; I'm a female business owner with revenue of more than $1M (just 3% of us accomplish this, www.womenpresidentsorg.com/about/facts); I'm a wife; I'm a mom who is infertile; and, last but certainly not least, I'm a human who almost died three times while in a medically-induced coma.

It's laughable, really. Through all of those experiences, and apparently, despite the best efforts of the universe, I still hadn't learned the lesson that stalked me for the ensuing months of dark nights after the fire. That lesson, the gift from the fire, is this: The realization that I am not in control of anything. I am only in control of the way I react.

It wasn't until that lesson really sank in, until I fully embraced the gift of it—and believe me, I fought hard against it—that I understood that I'd spent my entire life living an illusion. I had written and lived a life-long narrative based on the belief that I alone controlled my world.

Inviting and accepting the reality that I was not some all-knowing wizardess with one hand on my crystal ball and wielding my trusty magic wand with the other was, frankly, devastating. And terrifying. And liberating. Over the years, it's even become kind of magical. It is the biggest learning of my life in a lot of ways.

This is going to sound so corny, but I'm going to say it anyway. This gift really is like being the caterpillar in the cocoon and coming out of it as a butterfly. The world is ever so much more beautiful when you realize, when you truly get it; when you choose and intentionally decide on your own response, then you do control your own destiny.

Through fire, I had lost myself, and I had found myself.

The Opportunity to Choose

N ow, almost seven years later, I can totally and completely choose my own responses. I'm not perfect with it; of course, I have to be thoughtful about it. But I intentionally experience life differently. It's a practice. I've found it incredibly valuable to integrate this "no control" lesson into my day-to-day, rather than saving it for extreme (and sort of common, for me) circumstances like fires and comas.

I used to have a theory that most people don't think the way I do about control. Most of us don't realize our responses are a choice. Instead, we (collectively) automatically just experience. We don't think about what we're experiencing. We're just in the experience, whatever it is. The reaction is, "Okay, this is what's happening. I just have to deal with it." Well, my theory has been confirmed. Because when COVID-19 locked us down in 2020, I watched a metaphorical version of my fire happen to the world. Our collective illusion of control vanished. And we lost our shit.

Having my own personal intimacy with what it's like to be on a ventilator, I had an immediate and healthy respect for the coronavirus and its agenda. I had a bit of déjà vu. The universe was offering all of us a beautiful and terrifying opportunity to learn that we are not in control. It's so blindingly obvious. We can't control a virus. We can only control our response to it.

So, I wondered. Will we get it? As I watched, I thought, "I know it's possible to come out stronger on the other side of this." Of course, it's relatively easy for one individual like me to take a lesson and turn it into a practice from which I live my life. But could we do it collectively?

Maybe. I think we can—one person at a time. And I can help.

Hence this book.

A World on Fire

O kay, so it's fair if you're thinking, "Hey Andrea, wait a minute. Let me get this straight. You just spent a bunch of time explaining that the greatest learning of your life is that you don't control anything, and then you turn around and tell me that you wrote a book to tell the whole damn world how to get the lesson it took YOU so long to learn?"

The answer, and I'm laughing as I write this, is YES. Anybody who knows me will tell you that's how I roll.

As I said, along with the understanding that I control nothing came the certainty that I can – and definitely do – choose my own response to everything. This book is my response to what I see happening in the world right now. I believe it's my honor and responsibility to share my experience with the hope that others who are attracted to it might use it for their own learning and growth. Our individual growth adds to our collective understanding.

The pandemic, COVID-19, the coronavirus, is the world's version of my fire. I started writing this book a couple of months after the March 2020 lockdown. I can't tell you how fascinating it was to watch the people of the world—individually and collectively—begin to realize, just as I did, that there is no such thing as control. There is only our response to our circumstances. We had been handed one helluva big circumstance, one that threatened (and still threatens) our very lives and lifestyles, and we had no idea how to react to it.

I get that; I understand what it feels like to live under and with the threat of death and the terror of life-altering change. I've lived through tons of shit, and I'm always stronger on the other side of it.

Hence this book.

A Pandemic of Victim Mentality

Were you cheered by our collective reaction at the beginning of the pandemic? Remember how we were "all in this together?" Well, of course, that only lasted about 15 minutes. We're human. We're busy. We've lost jobs and dreams and people we love. We've lost our way of life. We've lost what some of us perceive as our freedoms.

And you know what? While the pandemic is a great equalizer in the fact that its agenda is to kill humans (and we're all human), it has also pulled back the curtain and exposed the many ways we are so deeply divided. Our differences—rather than our commonalities—became harshly spotlighted.

Once we got beyond that first 15 minutes of "Rah Rah, we're all in this together," we began to devolve into the stark realization that the world is out of control and we are powerless—powerless!—against it. So, what did we do? We went with it! We started pointing fingers and blaming each other. We still are, as I write this.

And ah! I recognized that feeling of powerlessness! I've had it (and used it) with great success in my life.

That feeling can lead to a victim mentality and I believe we are collectively deep in it.

I know this because choosing not to see myself as a victim of the things that happen to me is another gift of a lesson for me. I learned it from the experience of powerlessness that walked hand in hand with me as I was going through infertility treatments. I lived for a long time in that space, so I recognize it and its dangers.

When I talk about being in a victim mindset, I mean it's a thing. It's a way of life for many. To me, living in a victim mindset is operating with the belief that life happens to me, and I have no control over it. Watching our collective victim take hold during the pandemic has caused me to think that we live so much in victim—in the belief that "the world is out to get me and I can't do a damn thing about it"—that it's become an American value.

Please understand that I am not saying being victimized and being in victim mindset are the same thing. We can each be victims of the pandemic but allowing it to put us in a victim mindset is optional.

At one point during a political rally in late 2020, Donald Trump stood in front of a stadium full of his supporters and said, "We're all victims. Everybody here, all these thousands of people here tonight. They're all victims. Every one of you."

My response to that? In a victim mindset, we freely (and mostly unknowingly) cede our own power to others. Shit happens. All suffering happens. It's going to happen around us.

We are all victims of something. We have all been victimized in some way. Many of us are victims of racial or gender discrimination, of crime, of abuse, of violence, of bullying, of…the list is endless. We are not at fault for those experiences. But we are at choice and responsible for how we react to them. Believing and living in a victim mindset is a choice.

In truth, just as in the lesson about control, living in our own power is all about choosing our response. By choosing our responses—every single day, in every single moment—each of us chooses responsibility for what we're creating in our lives.

During my journey through the heavily loaded minefield that is infertility, I thought of myself as defective. I told people I was defective. I was in a victim mentality for sure, but it was also my unwillingness to move forward and past it, until I had an impetus to do so, that kept me in my own victim mentality.

A lot of people are like that. We're not necessarily individuals who are all-knowing and all being. We don't automatically tap into the part of our brain that questions our responses. Rather, we like to stew in our juices, in our shit. Shit's warm. It's warm. It feels good. We don't want to move. We don't move until it starts to stink.

Well, I think it stinks to live in a world that is comfortable choosing victim mentality and uncomfortable choosing responsibility—and therefore choosing ourselves and each other.

Hence this book.

Stronger on the Other Side

F or some reason, you found your way to this book. For many reasons already noted—not the least of which is my vision to live in a world full of people responsible for themselves and each other—I've found my way to write it.

People have asked me time and again to write a book. I didn't see the value in it until now. Now seems to be the perfect time to use my unique life and lessons as a conversation for change and growth in others, however they experience it.

For me, *Stronger on the Other Side* is about the befores and afters of my life, and how they've taught me lessons that created strength in me that I didn't have or hadn't yet tapped into. What's on the other side is a place of more acceptance of myself, a celebration of my voice, and the certainty that I own the power to use it all for good. The world is teaching me that my thoughts and insights matter. As do yours.

My podcast, *Lead Like a Woman,* celebrates and focuses on empowering women leaders to inspire other women through the stories of their lives and learning. I grew up in such a way that I didn't feel like I mattered, and that was more about being a female than anything else.

I didn't write this book exclusively for women, but it's ultimately about what women experience (so I hope you'll invite the men in your life to read it).

I believe it is my responsibility to take the experiences of my life and focus them through my lens so others can learn from them. This is me taking what I've learned and saying to you, "My friend, you don't have to experience all the shit I did. I'm happy to show you mine so you can use it as a map to get to a different place, or find an alternative action to take, or change your thinking." Without the shit.

In order to grow as individuals and as a collective whole, as women, as a nation, as a community, we have to be able to see the other side of the coin. I'm mixing metaphors now, but for us to change the world—and make no mistake, it's women who are shouldering the responsibility of that change—we have to be able to visualize something greater than ourselves.

Hence this book.

The Practice

As I said, choosing my response to whatever life throws my way has now become a practice. Through this book it's my hope that you can use my life experience to learn from and perhaps craft your own practice of choosing your response to the circumstances life hands you.

At the end of each section, you'll find reflective questions to ask yourself that are related a bit to my stories and lessons and an invitation that you might see your own experience in it. Where are you feeling voiceless in your life? What's keeping you from stepping into your own unique power? And I'll give you some of my personal practices that keep me at choice for my own responses.

It is my hope that you feel powerful. It's an amazing feeling. I'd like you to feel that you can do anything and know that even when the world tells you you're a victim of something, that you choose you. I'd like you to know that you and only you are in charge of your own life and the way you react to your challenges. The world doesn't do things to you. You respond to the things that are happening, and it's your choice how you do that. Just yours. Only yours.

In 2019 I wrote an article called "Leading Like a Woman" that became the 3rd most viewed article on LinkedIn. I ended it this way: "To the amazing women in my personal and professional life, thank you for the opportunity to be inspired and mentored by your leadership."

This book is me returning the favor. I'm eager to hear your stories and your learning. Please write me: andrea@strongerontheotherside.net.

Section 1: *Other*

"There is always the other side. Always." -Jean Rhys

The world will tell you that you're not enough. It will tell you that you can always do better, you should always try harder. It will say in a million ways that you're not the smartest, not the most driven, not the quickest. You'll spend so much time trying to prove yourself and it will be exhausting. You'll see things differently when you focus on how amazing you are rather than looking for where you feel that you're lacking. You are enough.

The Other Side of Other

I love words. One of the things I do for fun is play Scrabble online for about four hours a week. I'm in the top three percent in the country.

A magnetic Scrabble board hangs on the wall at our home. None of my family will play with me. In their view, I am "better than" or *"other* than" they are at playing and winning the game. When it comes to Scrabble, I am o*ther* to 97 percent of the country and 100 percent of my family.

I believe we are all some version of *other*. For fun, let's explore the word.

In 2017, Merriam-Webster.com entered other as a verb, with this explanation: *Other*, which we enter as an adjective, a noun, a pronoun, and an adverb, is increasingly being used as a verb meaning "to treat that culture as fundamentally different from another class of individuals, often by emphasizing its apartness.

The act and experience of *othering* is rampant in society and of course has been throughout human history. A very simplified current example is the finger-pointing that happens in the mask vs. no mask COVID-19 conversation. Those who wear a mask are *other* to those who don't, and vice versa.

I have a point here—and it's a good one. Bear with me. I love words. There are many of them in this book.

Some Version of *Other*

A s I said, I believe we are all some version of *Other*. I also believe we each understand what it feels like to be treated as "fundamentally different from another class of individuals."

Othering is a game of "less than" and "greater than." It's also about "good enough" and "not good enough." *Othering* marginalizes and minimizes groups and individuals.

In the summer of 2016, the Haas Institute for a Fair and Inclusive Society at the University of California, Berkeley published a document called Othering & Belonging: Expanding the Circle of Human Concern. From authors John A. Powell & Stephen Menendian: "We define *othering* as a set of dynamics, processes, and structures that engender marginality and persistent inequality across any of the full range of human differences based on group identities. Dimensions of othering include, but are not limited to, religion, sex, race, ethnicity, socioeconomic status (class), disability, sexual orientation, and skin tone. Although the axis of difference that undergird these expressions of othering vary considerably and are deeply contextual, they contain a similar set of underlying dynamics."

The authors also said, "The problem of the twenty-first century is the problem of othering. (It's a fascinating publication, and you can download it here if you'd like to know more. https://otheringandbelonging.org/wp-content/uploads/2016/07/OtheringAndBelonging_Issue1.pdf)

Anyway, I tell you all of this to make a point—well, several points. 1) I'm not just making this up. 2) I never want to the be the smartest person in the room (or the book in this case), so it is always my goal to make others smarter. And 3) It's important to me that women in particular understand that this is a problem we continue to face as we grow and gain power and equality.

Othering creates individual and collective consequences that ask us to make a choice about our experience of feeling and/or being *Othered*.

Also, important to keep in mind as you read my story is this: *Othering* is not always intentional, yet that does not lessen its impact.

Other Shit

I was mostly kidding about being seen as *other* because of my prowess in Scrabble. It's a silly little story and enormously miniscule when compared to the consequence and experience of what happens to people who are *Othered* individually and collectively, systemically and consistently.

Please notice that I used the word 'compare' here. *Othering* is about comparison—in all the ways society compares us to other and the ways we compare ourselves to *other*. I want to say emphatically that I am in no way comparing my *other* experiences to yours or yours to mine. I am fully aware that by many standards I am a financially secure, privileged white woman, and there is common opinion in the world that because of my status, my voice is not as valuable as those with deeper and uglier stories of ostracism.

I understand that.

Despite my status (or perhaps even because of it) my experience of *other* is commonplace and therefore may stand as a source of inspiration for many. As I said in the introduction, one of the reasons I wrote this book is to show you my shit in the hopes it will support you in getting through and learning from your own shit.

I will, by the end of this section, ask you to begin to examine where *other* shows up in your life, what it's creating for you, and how you're choosing to react to it.

Women are Other at Birth

L et me say that again. Women are other at birth. Simply because we are not male, we are born on the downside of other, meaning we have a climb ahead of us to get to the stronger side of it.

Of course, we don't know this in the cradle or during our first toddling steps into the rooms of a world owned mostly by men. It takes most of us years of watching and experiencing sexism, misogyny, gender inequalities and all of the other (see what I did there?) ways society disempowers and marginalizes women before we even realize there's something else available to us.

Just in case you think gender inequality is a done deal and doesn't deserve attention here in the 21st century, a 2020 study says otherwise. It is stunningly revealing. The Gender Social Norms Index released by the United Nations Development Programme (UNDP) found that "despite decades of progress in closing the equality gap between men and women, close to 90 percent of men and women hold some sort of bias against women."

Yes, you read that correctly. Ninety percent.

Further, "about half of the world's men and women feel that men make better political leaders, and over 40 percent feel that men make better business executives and that men have more right to a job when jobs are scarce. 28 percent think it is justified for a man to beat his wife."

I couldn't even speak when I read that, and anybody who knows me will tell you I can always speak (I was once put in a medical coma to shut me up, but that's Chapter 3).

Back to other. We each have our own individual stories that build into the collective story of this version of other, and, I believe, much to learn from them about how we can support each other on this particular journey.

My Version of Other

My journey with other begins in 1971. I was born Andrea Ellis to parents John and Janet, in Renton, Washington, a suburb of Seattle. My parents had adopted a son, my brother Ryan, seven months before I was born. My brother Aaron is three years younger than I am.

My dad is very much a traditionalist. We were part of a right wing, conservative Christian church and philosophy. In hindsight, I would call it almost cult-like. The subtext of my childhood was "be quiet, don't put yourself out there too much, don't make waves."

Before I go much further into my childhood, I want to be clear. I love my parents. Their story is not mine, and mine is not theirs. My parents loved me and raised me the best they could, and they still love me in the best ways they can. Whether they and their love show up in the manner I want it to doesn't matter. They love me as they love me. The only response I can choose, and change is my own.

In many ways, I had an ideal 1970s childhood. I learned early, though, that I was not like the rest of my family and I was mostly not like my friends. I was, as Merriam Webster defines other, "fundamentally different from another class of individuals."

I didn't know it, of course. It was what it was. I had no other frame of reference. The fact that I was compared to my brothers, the fact that I didn't measure up to my brothers in some ways, was normal.

In the belief system of my family of origin—despite the fact that my mom had her own career—the message to me was that girls weren't meant to do anything, really. We were supposed to just find a husband who would take care of us and in return, we'd have the kids and be good moms and clean the house and cook. In the seventies and early eighties, I didn't have any clue that I could be something different.

Occasionally one of my podcast guests on my *Lead Like a Woman* show says something like, "Oh, I grew up with every possibility in the world. Women could do anything!" I cannot relate to that. That is not what my world told me. My world told me to be quiet. My world told me to be subservient. My world, at the time, told me my job was to be a mom and a wife. That's who I was supposed to be. That's what the church told me, that's what my parents told me. So that's what I thought.

I Goofed. Again.

I have a confession to make. This is not my first book. I wrote my first book when I was six years old—one of those fabric-covered projects many of us have gathering dust in a box somewhere.

My book was called, "I Goofed. I Goofed. I Goofed. I Goofed Again, Like Always." That title is totally indicative of my entire childhood and how I felt. Again, I was six at the time.

By six years old, I had developed the idea—and this is something that's still true in my life today—that I always had to live up to expectations. And if I didn't live up to expectations, I was downgraded in the eyes of my parents. And I'd get in trouble.

I tried really hard to be what my parents wanted me to be. I believed what they believed in and almost always did what I was told. I was not somebody who pushed boundaries then.

My experience of other in my childhood created an unconscious victim mindset for me. That mindset showed up as "I am voiceless," and, "My voice doesn't matter." Or, "My voice gets me in trouble" (and it did). I felt that no matter what I did, it would never be good enough.

I lost the district spelling bee when I was in the sixth grade. I failed on the word chifforobe, which I now forever know how to spell (and there are three accepted spellings). After I missed the word, I remember standing on stage, thinking, "OMG, I don't want to talk to my dad. He's going to be so disappointed." I was worried about seeing both of my parents after I lost, because I hadn't lived up to the expectation that I would win at the district level and then go on to the state competition. I was devastated.

I didn't have a lot of fun growing up. I did what was expected of me. Talking back wasn't allowed. No sassing. So, any time I had an opinion, it was looked at as sass. This was true only for me, though. My brothers got away with using their voices.

I became what Ryan called a "goody two shoes." I became a people pleaser. My goal in life was to get accolades and praise from my parents. And that was hard to get, so occasionally I acted out.

Ryan and I walked to school together every day. It was probably only a half-mile away, but once in a while my mom would drive past us on her way to drop off my little brother, Aaron, at daycare. I used to get so angry when she passed us! Couldn't she see us? We would always ask for a ride, because really, if she's driving by, why not?

As I saw it, the pecking order of favor in our family was Aaron first (he could get away with anything), then Ryan, and then me. Because Ryan and I were so close in age (seven months) we were constantly compared to each other and I felt that I always came up short. On a particular day when my mom drove past us, I guess I was fed up, because I got angry and yelled and screamed and called her a bitch.

Well, I had tattled on Ryan for playing with matches recently, and he was still mad at me about it, so he got back at me by telling on me the minute my mom got home from work that day. I ended up having to write "I will not call my mother names," 1000 times.

No sassing, and no swearing. I goofed again. I clearly had a voice at this point in my childhood, but even so, I felt unheard and unseen. Voiceless.

Cookie Dough and Judgment

Despite our sibling battles, Ryan and I were very close. We still are. Ryan and I were latchkey kids, which is a term coined in the 80s (from Wikipedia: A latchkey kid is a child who returns to an empty home after school or a child who is often left at home with no supervision because his or her parents are away at work).

We would do things like eat SpaghettiOs out of the can. Or, I would make a big batch of cookie dough and we would eat it raw with spoons while we watched after school specials.

Ryan was well-liked at school, and he was definitely more popular than I was. Though we fought and tattled on each other like all kids, he was my protector in a lot of ways. I was kind of a nerd. I was the quiet kid.

There was one student in fourth grade, K., who was my nemesis – my total nemesis. She made fun of me. She made fun of my clothes. She called me a nerd. My family didn't have a whole lot of money, so I wore clothes that weren't stylish and stylish was expected in our school. Plus, I was growing like a weed. I was the tallest kid in school in fifth grade – taller even than some of my teachers.

I was awkward in my own body. And then my family made fun of me, too. They teased me about the way I walked, about the size of my nose, about other things I couldn't control. And it hurt.

I used to be utterly fearful that other people wouldn't accept me, that they would think I was fat, or ugly, or not well-spoken. My biggest fear was always being judged and coming up short.

The Nerd

On the other hand, at school I was the kid who was teacher's pet. I knew the answers, so I'd raise my hand and shout them out. I liked being smart. I loved it. It fed me, in some way, to feel smart in class. However, at home I felt better accepted if I was quiet.

I could be a smartass sometimes, like when I got kicked out of Girl Scouts in fourth grade. I was in Juniors, which is a step above Brownies, and I didn't much like our troop leader or her daughter. I doubted everything the troop leader would tell us to do. I'd say, "Hey, why don't we do it this way? My way is better," and questioned her authority all the time. Well, she was friends with my mom and told her she thought it was best that I leave the troop. My mom pulled me out.

I was beginning to find my voice. Yet I was also afraid to admit I was smart because I didn't want anyone judging me for it. I tested into the gifted program in fourth grade, but my teacher told my parents he didn't think I was ready for it.

I tested again in fifth grade and in sixth grade moved to the gifted classroom across town. I made a whole new group of friends, and I got to be whoever I wanted to be in this new setting, including being on stage to perform to "Eye of the Tiger" and "Leader of the Pack."

It was awesome. I had fun. I remember my dad asking me, "Do you really want to be on stage?" It was a reminder of my growing-up subtext for girls: "Don't put yourself out there too much."

In middle school I was bussed to the high school for math because I'd already completed the middle school math requirements. I was in high school algebra in seventh grade.

I did my pre-SATs in seventh grade because we had an option to do that through the gifted program. I scored a perfect score on language arts and high scores in the math and science portions as well. My parents received a letter from the University of Washington inviting me to learn about the University's program that allowed kids with high PSAT's to go straight to college.

I was super excited about the program. I felt like I'd found my tribe, my people, someplace where I fit in. I wasn't a nerd! I so badly wanted to attend the program, but my parents couldn't afford it.

I was absolutely devastated because for once I had felt like I belonged, like I wasn't *other*.

Confusing Dichotomies

As I look back, I realize my early life was full of dichotomies that may have fueled my fears and confusion and contributed to feelings of being unheard and *other*.

I developed breasts early and was wearing a bra by fourth grade. A boy in my class snapped my bra. I went home and told my mom and she said, "He just likes you." That was how she grew up. Forgive the boys. It's not their fault.

I had women in my life whose lives contrasted with my family's strict religious belief system. As I said, my mom worked out of the house at a time when a lot of the other moms didn't. And my grandmothers were badass strong role models for me.

My Grandma Gerry took me to get my ears pierced for my 13th birthday. My dad's reaction was, "Only streetwalkers and loose women have pierced ears." I said, "But your mother has them!" He replied, "Well, she makes her own decisions."

Huh? He adored his mother.

I remember being in the car with my dad and hearing him debase women with comments like, "That woman doesn't know how to drive." Or "Stupid broad."

I overheard a conversation (actually it was an argument) between my parents after my mom graduated with her master's degree in school administration. She was the principal at a local christian elementary school. My mom said to my dad, "I'd like to go for my PhD, John." He said, "No wife of mine will ever have more education than I have."

It's no wonder I remember wanting to be a man.

Getting Through
the Unhappy

When I was 14, I wanted to kill myself. I was so sad, and it was a deep-down sorrow. Today I might call it grief.

I was in a bad place. I was teased a lot. I was the brain. I was the nerd, and people made fun of me. I had no friends at school. None. My friends were all church youth group friends, and they lived far away, so I only saw them at church.

I stole a bottle of my mom's sleeping pills and I walked around with them in my pocket, thinking, "If I just take these, I'll be okay." I didn't feel like I was necessarily making a choice to die. I just wanted to stop being sad.

My brother Ryan and I had a conversation that tipped him off that something was wrong. He went to my parents, which from an adult perspective is exactly what you want him to do, obviously. I realize now that if I hadn't wanted someone to step in, I wouldn't have told him, but I didn't recognize that at the time.

My parents brought over the youth minister—Cory—from our right-wing conservative Christian church. I told him that I was battling with feeling like I didn't matter. I felt teased. I felt demeaned. I didn't have a voice in my family or anywhere else because women weren't supposed to be heard. I felt that I wasn't allowed to have an opinion because I was female.

Cory and I had a long conversation—like for six hours—talking about where I was and what I needed and who I wanted to be and who I couldn't be. As we talked, I realized that I did have a choice and that I didn't have to go down the path I was considering. I could choose life versus death. I could choose—not happiness because I wasn't at all happy at that time in my life—but I could choose to get through the unhappy.

That conversation brought me to a realization that it was okay for me to feel sad, but not okay to pull the trigger on myself. Cory said what I needed to hear: "Andrea, it's going to be okay, you're going to figure this out. Maybe not today, maybe not tomorrow, maybe not next year, but at some point in time, things will get better."

That conversation showed me the possibility that I could matter and that I actually had a strong voice. I just didn't feel like I could use it.

(Funny side story. Cory officiated at my wedding to my husband Eric in 1994. Cory wanted me to say "obey" in the ceremony. I didn't. And he wanted to introduce us as Mr. and Mrs. Eric Heuston. That didn't happen either. I had learned the power of my voice by then.)

And by the way, I still hate being teased. I don't take it well at all. Half the time Eric doesn't know what to do with me because Eric loves to tease. Sometimes I let him get away with it but sometimes my gut reaction is to take exception and be and feel offended by it.

I Figured It Out

C ory was so right when he said I'd figure it out. When I was 16, I literally left my family, my school, my church and my life behind and fled across the ocean to Europe.

I found out about the Rotary foreign student exchange program during my sophomore year in high school. My French teacher, Marty Gale, encouraged me, as did Dr. Kirby Unti, the pastor at the Lutheran church, who was the head of the Rotary program.

I loved French, I was good at languages (I speak seven of them with varying degrees of fluency) and I desperately wanted to go to France, so I applied for the exchange program and didn't tell my parents at first. When we got to the point that they had to approve it, it was quite a conversation because it was a costly program, and it was for an entire year.

I did end up going, obviously, but not to France, because I was highly allergic to the pollens and plants that I would encounter there. My second choice was Scandinavia because my mom is half-Swedish. I went to Denmark.

Wow, I Can Do This

The first family I was with in Denmark wasn't a good placement. Denmark's Rotary exchange system, at the time, required that families take in three students for every child they send out, and the mom of my exchange family didn't really want me there. We had a difficult relationship, and I knew it wasn't going to work. I needed to get out.

Except I didn't know how. I was 16 years old, had been in this foreign country for eight weeks, and didn't yet speak the language. I had no freaking clue what to do. So, I called my mom. From a pay phone.

She said, "Andrea, you have to go to the counselor." Well, I didn't want to go to the counselor because they were friends with my exchange family. But in that moment, I realized it was up to me. I had to use my voice if I wanted to make this happen.

I went to the counselor and he said, "We've had complaints about this family before. You're moving in with us." And that's what happened. I spent a tense hour at the host family's home when I went to pack up my things. She obviously was not happy with me. But that was when I realized I could step up and do things for myself, that I had control over my situation. I could do this.

Denmark

Denmark was culture shock for me in many ways. I was certainly *Other*, but everybody wanted to know me! I became the popular kid. Never in my life had I been the popular kid. All of a sudden, I had attention that I hadn't expected or even known was possible in my life in the states.

I was very independent in Denmark, in a socialist culture that was vastly different than the culture in which I had grown up. I quickly began to see how oppressive my world was, how patriarchal home was, compared to Denmark, which was already making huge strides toward equal pay for women.

The whole thing was fascinating to me, this young woman who thought of herself as a Republican simply because my Dad was a Republican. I realized, then, that maybe the United States wasn't the be all and end all I had understood it to be, that there were varied systems of government and distinct systems of belief that served people differently and effectively.

I created a new version of family in Denmark as well. I really connected with one host family, the Jensens, and maintain those relationships to this day. Besides my other host families, I met Karina, the sister of my heart. Our deep connection is hard to describe, so I'll simply say that Karina always feels like home to me, no matter where we are or what we're doing. She's my soul sister. She's still my dearest friend on earth, other than my husband and my dog.

After a year in the program and a lifetime's worth of new experiences, I was a completely changed Andrea.

I wept the day I left Denmark. That memory is like a movie ending in my head. I'm the star, of course, this nerd girl from the U.S., who considered suicide and had few friends in her former life back home. I see myself walking to the plane, with 50 of my friends and Danish family members who've shown up at the airport to see me off, and someone drapes the Danish flag over my shoulders.

I went to Denmark and found my voice. I discovered that I could make my own decisions, believe in the things that I wanted to believe in, and see the world through different eyes.

It was the most pivotal experience I could have had as a young person. I became who I was supposed to be. I don't know who I would have been without it, but I sure like who I am now.

Home

I had found my voice in such a way that I was able to convince my parents and Karina's dad that she should become an exchange student in the U.S., so she joined me at my home a month later and we spent our senior year together.

She lived at my house and it really helped me transition because, although I had left a part of me in Denmark, I also brought parts of me back. Having her with me made the transition a lot easier. It was a softer place to fall with Karina here, because my welcome wasn't particularly warm.

When I left the U.S., I was the "good daughter," and I came back with a very different idea of the world and a broader view of society in general. I was more outgoing and outspoken. It was also a shock to my parents. My Dad will still say to this day that he regrets letting me go to Denmark. He had a really hard time with the fact that I loved Denmark so much and that I'd grown up in the time that I'd left.

Denmark is where I learned to think for myself. I had come to know who I was and who I could be. I had discovered that I didn't have to fall in line and always do what my parents expected me to.

My church friends didn't really embrace me when I came back, either. I had left a good Christian girl who recited bible verses and went to youth group. My dear friend Mandy, who I've known since I was 12 and is still one of my best friends, has said, "Andrea, I was so bad to you for those two or three years after you came back. I just didn't think you were Christian anymore."

Okay, I admit that was possibly because I had stopped wearing a bra. My core group of Christian friends couldn't handle it. I did lose friends over it. But I had changed. Denmark was a much freer country, and therefore I was as well.

I was different. It wasn't that I was necessarily sexually active, but I had a freer mentality about sex and sexuality that did not match with the Christian church whatsoever.

Adulting

I adulted pretty quickly after I returned home. It was 1988. I had a year left of high school, but I only needed one class to graduate. I got an internship job at my dad's company as a technical illustrator.

I was accepted at Whitman College (aka the Ivy League of the West), Radcliffe and the University of Washington. I was given early entrance to Whitman, decided I was going to go there and super excited about it. I had a $9K academic scholarship; back then tuition was $14K.

The summer before I was to begin college, my dad was laid off from his job. My mom had taken a year off to complete her graduate degree and they pulled me aside and said, "You can't go to Whitman. We don't have the money."

I tried everything to fix the situation. I tried to get work study but didn't qualify because the parental income requirements were based on the previous year. I had to decline Whitman's offer and scholarship.

I moved out, got my own apartment, and worked at the company that I had been interning with full time. I put myself through community college, then went to the University of Washington and graduated in 1997. It took me longer to graduate than most, but I paid for every penny of college myself.

In May of 1995, the company I worked for—the same company I'd started working for as an intern in 1988—was acquired by a French firm.

I was 24 years old, had worked myself up to be the head of the creative services department, and had a team of six under me. I was asked to lay them all off, which I did. And then the next day, they laid me off. I didn't see that writing on the wall because I'd had no experience.

Two days later they called me and said, "Andrea, we need you to come back and bring one of your team members. We have to roll out the entire brand change. The head company out of France isn't going do it for us."

I said, "Hold, please," and drove myself down to the state capital in Olympia the next day and got a business license. I called the company back and said, "Sure, I'll come back, but you'll be paying me and my colleague, Sandy, through my company, Artitudes Layout and Design."

I founded what is now Artitudes Design with $5,000 I borrowed from my grandmother to purchase a computer, a printer, and business cards. I didn't ever want to put my destiny into somebody else's hands again.

And I haven't. I was done being *Othered*.

Oh Shit, I Othered Myself

I owned Artitudes Design for more than a decade before I really owned it in the strongest sense of the word. I owned the shit I was still carrying from feeling o*thered* in my youth.

Even after founding and running my own company for years, I had gotten pretty adept at internalizing my early lessons and o*thering* myself. I didn't really believe I was good enough, that I could perform to expectations.

Until my attorney told me I needed to incorporate, I thought of myself as just this little sole proprietor. I was a woman doing her own thing. I was a mom. It was a mom-job.

And then it wasn't.

When I incorporated, my mentor recommended that the first thing I do was get into Vistage (Vistage is a global executive coaching organization). I argued that it was too expensive, but I did join their lowest tier, which was not the CEO group, but a group for businesses that served other businesses.

I moved up to the CEO group fairly quickly. I was incorporated for only a year when my revenues hit $1M, so it was a fast move, and I was blessed to be in a group coached by a man named Ron Kranz.

By this time, I'd been running my business for 12 years, and had been consistently calling myself something with "creative" in the title. At the time, I think I was "Creative Principal." Ron said, "Andrea, you need to be the CEO. And I said, "No, Ron. A CEO is an old white man in a suit." I said this, by the way, to an old white man in suit.

I wouldn't even name myself president at first. And I had to, in my mind, get to president before I could get to CEO because I had these images in my head of what they were, and they weren't me. I was a young woman. Who the hell was I to think I could be a CEO?

Through Vistage, I sat in a group of males, and was the only woman in the room. Every single male in this peer group called himself CEO. It took me three or four meetings with them for me to say to Ron that I was ready to be President. I saw that these men were doing the same things I was doing, but in different ways. And I had valuable, valid ideas that powerful men listened to for the first time in my life. In some ways, I felt validated. I could become the President of my company.

It took me a year and a half to two years after that initial conversation to change my title to CEO. Ron was my business coach for years. He walked me through the value I was adding. At one point he said to me, "Andrea, it's just a title. But it's a title that will open doors. You can believe it now or you can believe it later, but you need to embrace that title."

I believe it. I am Andrea Heuston, CEO of Artitudes Design Inc.

Stronger on the Other Side of Other

As a female, I was born on the downside of *other* and it took me a long time to climb to the stronger side of it.

I had to look inside myself to realize that I was worthy of choosing CEO, of being that person. And for me, that created a level of strength I didn't know I had. I knew I knew my stuff. I am an expert at certain things, and I am really good at what I'm good at. I can talk a terrific game and I can be a resource for people. My voice is respected.

There's a reason I was able to start a business just based on who I was and the value I gave clients, because I was really good at what I did. However, I never fully believed that I had a seat at the male table.

I told myself I did, though. Because sometimes you just have to name it to tame it. You say it, so you become it. It's my way to finally own my voice and power.

I couldn't become CEO until I could redefine CEO my way. I'm the CEO of my life, of my family and of my company. I'm not an old white man in a suit. I don't operate like a man. I don't lead like a man. I lead like a woman.

It was all about perspective – about realizing that it's okay to have a different definition. It was that realization that finally convinced me. And this sad fact, which I tout all the time: Only three percent of female-owned business make it above the $1M mark. My business is in that three percent, which in some ways also makes me *other*. It also makes me a fucking rockstar.

Practice

C hoosing my response to whatever life throws my way has now become a practice. At the end of each section, you'll find four questions and a ten-minute exercise to help you identify opportunities for active choice in your life. Use your responses as a mantra or reminder when you're faced with a situation similar to the section experience.

Your Active Choice

Choose to Own Your *Other*

What does it look like for you to own this experience, to be responsible for your response to the experience?

Questions

- What's your version of *other*?
- Where in your life are you voiceless?
- Have you created a victim mindset from your experience of being *othered*? Are you *othering* yourself? (That's a bonus question.)
- What have you gotten from your experience of *other* that you couldn't have gotten any other way?

Your 10-minute exercise:

Go online and read about whatever culture or group or individual that is *other* in your mind. We all have them. Choose your opportunity to explore your biases.

Have extra time? This is fun.

https://implicit.harvard.edu/implicit/education.html

Section 2: Broken

"A wounded deer leaps highest." -Emily Dickinson

First, you're going to be okay. You will make it through – through this, through everything. It won't always seem that way, but if you choose happiness, if you choose positivity, if you choose your own path, you'll be okay. You are enough.

The Other Side of Broken

R ight up front at the beginning of this chapter I want to say this clearly, because it's one of the reasons I've struggled over the years with writing this book: I don't ever want anyone—for fuck's sake—to feel sorry for me. When I do keynote speeches or other presentations and have shared my stories, a common question is, "How are you still standing?" My answer is always, "Oh my God, I'm stronger than I've ever been."

I am strong because I was broken. Or at least because I saw myself that way.

The Broken Side
of Broken

E ric and I married in 1994, and we started talking about having kids about four years in. Some of our friends were down that path already and we thought we'd explore it, too. I was 27, Eric was 26 and kids just seemed like the natural next step for us.

I'm stereotyping now, but I believe most of us think getting pregnant is just going to be easy. I remember thinking, "Okay, well, here we go. Next month we'll be pregnant."

I came by that belief naturally, being raised in my religious household where sex before marriage was a no-no, and reinforced by the knowledge that my dad had had a surprise baby and forced first marriage when he was a young man in college.

My belief was that the minute Eric and I tried to have kids we would get pregnant, it would be a no-brainer, and it would be done. This getting pregnant thing must be a breeze, right? It must just happen.

Yeah. It didn't. It absolutely didn't happen that way.

Because I was defective.

But I Could Control it, Right?

A t that time in my life, I still wanted to control everything. Before I knew I was defective, I was my usual get 'er done, cheerleader self: "Alright, let's go, let's do this! We're gonna have a baby! We'll have a kid by next year! Yeah! We're old enough, but we're still young enough to have fun with this!"

It turned out I couldn't control it, and it wasn't so much fun.

We tried without success for about a year before we decided to begin exploring what was going on. We started doing things like checking my basal body temperature, so we'd know when I was ovulating and fertile. I'd always had issues with my periods. They were brutal and painful and would put me in bed somedays, but at the time we didn't really think anything of it.

I made an appointment with my OB-GYN, who put me on Clomid, which modulates estrogen and is often the first step in getting pregnant. The protocol at the time was Clomid for six months, and if nothing happened, we'd move to the next step.

Hot flashes happened, but I did not get pregnant.

We moved on to seeing a fertility specialist. We originally started with my OB-GYN, but after a year and a half of trying, I had to drag myself there for appointments. Seeing pregnant bellies and newborn babies in the waiting room was much too frustrating and sad. It made it hard for me to continue.

Once a Month Death

In 18 months, I'd gone from excited and whole to feeling depressed and defective. The one thing that I can say about infertility in general is that it was like a death every month when I didn't get pregnant. Each month I was primed for life, and each month I grieved the life that didn't take hold and grow.

It absolutely mentally and emotionally took a toll on me, particularly because my early life had taught me that having children was the natural course for a woman. It's what I was meant to do. I was supposed to bear children. I was not living up to expectations. In essence, at my emotional core, I felt like I'd goofed. Again. And again.

In the meantime, my friend Kelly, who I'd been close with since we were 12, had gotten pregnant in her first month of trying. When Kelly's daughter, Joleen, was six months old and I was deep in the throes of my infertility journey, Kelly called me in tears. "WHAT is wrong?" I asked. She said, "I'm pregnant again and it's too soon. I'm not ready to have another baby right now."

I hung up, devastated. I was so very sad that I couldn't be happy for her or even help her on her journey. We're all good now and our friendship is lovely. But I simply couldn't be with her then. My infertility overshadowed everything else in my life.

Old Eggs

We chose to try a fertility clinic in downtown Seattle and started the next steps, one of which was clearing my fallopian tubes. They put me on an operating table and shot water and dye through my tubes. It was one of the most painful things I've ever experienced. Eric said I practically levitated off the table.

What we learned in the process—and was really confirming for me—is that it was me that was broken, not Eric. He was fertile. I just could not get pregnant.

One of the doctors told me that I would have been really fertile if I'd gotten pregnant at 12, that my eggs were old by the time I was 22. I said, (I can be a bit of a smartass as I mentioned) "That's helpful. Thanks for that. I really appreciate it."

We tried working with my old eggs for over a year through a series of Intrauterine Insemination (IUI) procedures. I took a bevy of fertility drugs that caused a 50-pound weight gain and I still couldn't get pregnant.

This was back before social media was a thing, and I'd found a website and chat from the InterNational Council on Infertility Information Dissemination (INCIID). It was the one place I could share my story with women who understood it, and they could share theirs. It was fascinating and fabulous and scary and sad, all at the same time.

We had decided by that time to look for a specialist in Invitro Fertilization (IVF). I asked for referrals on INCIID and found one of the foremost fertility doctors in the country. Dr. Kevin Sullivan came highly recommended, and we decided IVF with him was our next step.

By this time, I was nearing 30, feeling like a defective old pin cushion, and really, like this was never going to happen.

Gambling on One Round

Y ou know, married couples either get closer
together over infertility or are split wide apart.
Although it didn't feel like it at times, it truly brought
Eric and me together.

During this part of the journey, I had near constant
blood draws and injections. Even my veins were tired of
it. They started rolling away. One day I had blood taken
from my forehead, and another day from my foot. Those
were the only veins they could find. Eric gave me shots
in my butt and shots in my stomach area for months on
end, just so that we could create eggs to have a baby. It
was a difficult, difficult time but we did it because we
both really wanted kids. We wanted to be parents.

We knew we could afford exactly one round of IVF.
Twenty years ago, IVF cost around $20K and was not
covered by insurance. So, we sold things. We saved

pennies, we did everything we possibly could to get the money together, including borrowing from my parents, which was something we never thought we'd have to do.

IVF affected my body strangely. My ovaries kind of blew up with eggs which was an unusual response for someone with old eggs. They'd harvested eggs from me before, but not to the same degree.

On the day of insemination, I had seven fertilized eggs. None of them had made it to the blastocyst stage but the doctors still thought they might. So, they put all seven of those almost-embryos back into my body and waited.

And.

Not. A. Single. One. Took.

We Got Nothing

I was so utterly devasted I don't think I talked to anyone for weeks. We'd spent $20,000 and years of our lives. The physical, mental, and emotional toll was brutal. And we got nothing from it. That's how we felt.

The doctors said, well, you know, you can try again in a year, things are improving all the time. Another round was not in our financial or emotional budgets.

Of course, during this entire time I was talking with my Danish friend-like-a-sister Karina who was by then a mother (her oldest was born on my birthday) and living with her husband Dan in England. I kind of lost my mind with her over the phone after the failed IVF and she said, "Andrea, Dan and I have talked and if you want to come here, I will give you my eggs."

I have tears in my eyes as I write this because it's still the kindest, most amazing thing anyone's ever said to me: "I will give you my eggs."

Eric and I had a serious discussion about it. To make it work, we would have either had to become citizens of the UK or pay out of pocket, plus pay for our life in the U.S. At the very least I would have to stay overseas for six months.

We talked a lot, toyed with it, wondered what it would be like to have a kid who was ours and not ours at the same time. I would carry a baby that was Karina and Eric's. How does that work in the future? There were so many difficult questions.

Eventually, we decided we had to turn down Karina's amazing offer. We just couldn't make it work logistically.

It was October of 2000 when we decided to give it up. We were done.

Dark and Powerless

I went to a pretty deep and dark place for a long time. The voice in my head, which was speaking directly from my upbringing, said a woman was supposed to have a child and stay at home to parent that child.

I couldn't do the one thing—give birth to my baby—that I was put on earth to do. And I couldn't do anything about it. God knows I'd tried everything. Of course, it wasn't my fault. It wasn't anybody's fault. But I'd created a victim story around it and blamed myself anyway. I believed it and I lived in it.

I lost some of my sense of self during that time. I'm not a shy person, but I became more introverted. I became more dependent on other people, and I worried more about what other people thought of me.

For five years, I told people I was defective. I actually said those words. "I can't have a baby. I'm defective." "Um, sorry, husband. You shouldn't be with me if you want a family." I wore my pain and brokenness on my sleeve, like a blinking badge of honor. See, I fucked up. I goofed again. It's all my fault. I became my limiting belief. I beat myself up instead of loving myself.

I know now that I unintentionally chose—and it was a choice, albeit unconscious—to think of myself as broken. As defective. As a victim of my circumstances. Was it an understandable reaction? Yes. I was exhausted. Tired to my pin-cushioned bones. Beat down.

One of the women in the INCIID chat told me that I was not meant to be a parent. She said, Andrea, "God is telling you that because you can't give birth, you shouldn't have kids. You shouldn't be a parent."

Remember what I said in the introduction about staying in our shit because it's warm and cozy and familiar? Well, I held onto that shit—to be on the broken side of broken—until well after we had our kids.

I had gotten comfortable feeling powerless. And I would stay that way until I could admit to myself the possibility of choosing something even more powerful.

Adoption

My friends have often heard me say that I wouldn't wish infertility on my worst enemy. Well, adoption is no picnic either.

It wasn't long before we decided to move in that direction. With several adopted family members, including my brother Ryan and my grandmother, it was a natural progression for me. Of course, people in our family and friend circles had their own opinions about it, but I'll just share Eric's because it's my favorite. When someone asked him if he really wanted to open up his family to a child that's not his blood, he said, "My wife is my family, and she's not my blood, either." So there.

We went to an adoption fair at a local hospital and were matched right away with an attorney we really liked. We thought we'd go for a private adoption and avoid going through an agency. There's a cost and process differential that felt right to us at the time. I'm sure you can imagine how excited we were when we matched with a birth mom right away. But, when she was about three weeks away from giving birth, she backed out.

We were torn apart all over again.

Despite it, we moved forward. On the advice of some friends we met through an adoption support group, we joined an agency in Spokane, which is about five hours away where we live, just outside of Seattle.

By January we were matched again, but before I share more about that, I have to say that the whole process of getting to that point rubbed me the wrong way and pissed me off. We basically had to create a portfolio of our lives, a marketing tool to sell ourselves as potential parents.

I mean, you know, the world is full of people who conceive and give birth every day. There are no parenting requirements for them. It's fair, too, to say that we all know people who probably shouldn't be parents, for various reasons, and they have kids without restriction. And then there are people like us who cannot have babies and must also learn to jump through all the hoops required to get approval to adopt a baby. I'm not saying it shouldn't be that way, I'm just saying it infuriated me.

We actually hired an adoption consultant, so we'd know all the right answers. We didn't want to say the wrong thing (such as we believe in spanking…we don't, btw) and have some stranger decide we couldn't have a baby. We did a home study, provided credit reports, financials for the last five years, gave references, and on and on. It was absolute insanity.

But by January we were matched with two birth moms and the agency didn't give us a choice. They said, this birth mother came in first, so this is who you're matched with. Come over and meet her.

S, the Birth Mother

I'm going to refer to our birth mother simply as 'S' for the sake of privacy. S was three months pregnant at the time we met her. Her grandmother was very instrumental in creating a safe space for this adoption. S's mother had been adopted and was pretty anti-adoption and not supportive of it. Her grandmother, however, was utterly behind it.

Now, S had a backstory. I've learned over the years to take everything she says with a nod and a smile and an awareness of "Who knows what's true?" She told us that she had been kicked out of the house by her mom when she was ten and had lived on the streets ever since. She was 19.

We worked really hard on a relationship with her. I went over to Spokane (a five-hour drive) for doctor's appointments. S had a done a full background study that's designed to ensure that everyone is informed and aware of all situations and that the adoption will go through and all will be well. As we had already learned, it's heartbreaking for everyone involved when something happens to stop it at the last minute.

When S was eight months along, we got a call from the state. They told us that somehow some arrest records had been overlooked and that S had been drunk while she was pregnant. And, they said, we know she uses drugs, but we don't know which ones. As soon as I got off the phone, the agency called me and said you may want to reconsider this adoption.

Eric and I had already named the baby. I'd been to every doctor's appointment, and because it was an adoption and S was high risk, we'd seen our son multiple times through ultrasound. We already felt that we were his parents. Eric and I spent about 48 hours talking, discussing, and thinking. We called the agency back and said we wanted to move forward.

And then Aidan was born.

Aidan

I remember that morning so vividly. It was early—6 a.m.—on June 28 (Aidan was due on July 10). I was feeling sick with a super sore throat and was planning to work from home.

Eric had already left the house for work and five minutes later, the phone rang. It was S. She said, "I'm in labor. I'm leaving for the hospital. How soon can you get here?"

I called Eric, who was at the coffee stand across town, and he said, "I'm turning around. I'll call my boss." He got home, we threw on clothes, grabbed a bag, and made the five-hour drive to Spokane in three and half hours. We averaged a hundred miles an hour. Thank God we didn't get stopped.

We arrived at 12:02 p.m. and Aidan was born at 12:14 p.m. I held one of S's legs while she gave birth to Aidan. Eric cut the cord, they handed the newborn to me. And we had a baby.

I have the first photo (we have an album for Aidan) of Aidan, S, and me. We're both looking at the camera and tears are just streaming down our faces.

S didn't want Aidan in her room, and they wouldn't let us in the nursery. We had to get a lawyer and petition to be allowed in. I remember quite clearly another baby boy born the same day, who was side-by-side with Aidan in the nursery. His birth mother had abandoned him, and this baby had nowhere to go. I said to Eric, and I was serious, "We've got to take them both." Of course, they wouldn't let us do that. I never did find out what happened to that baby.

Six months later the adoption was finalized in court. According to Washington state law, during the first six months, the birth mother can change her mind and come take the child away. We were completely and totally

bonded to Aidan. Thank God S didn't make
that choice.

There have been interesting developments ever
since, but that's the story of how we got Aidan.

Hi. Do You Want Another Baby?

I always sent yellow roses to S on Aidan's birthday. When he was one, she got yellow roses. When he was two, she got yellow roses.

By this time, Aiden, was a miracle. He walked one day and ran the next, right before his first birthday. He hardly ever crawled. He was communicating with us in sign language by six months old. He knew milk, more, please, thank you, and Mom at six months. By nine months old, he had words. Aidan was a crazy smart child.

When Aidan turned three, I couldn't find S. We had lost her, which meant she was likely living on the streets again. So, I called her grandmother, Mary, and said, "Mary, I am trying to find S. I'd like to send her flowers, as I always do." She said, "Just a minute, Andrea." I thought she was going to get S's change of address for me, but S picked up the phone.

I wasn't prepared for that at all, or for the next words out of S's mouth. "Hi Andrea. Do you want another baby?" I wondered if she was talking about her daughter that she'd gotten pregnant with six months after Aidan was born.

I said, "Um, well, tell me what's going on?" And S said, "I'm pregnant. It's a boy and the baby is due on August 27." This was early June of 2004.

Well, August 27th was our 10th wedding anniversary, and without pausing to hang up the phone and call Eric, I said, "Yes, of course we'd love to have another baby."

I got off the phone with her, called Eric and said, "We're going to have a baby boy." He replied, "Andrea, I did not think that was possible. What are you talking about?"

Well, we got in the car that weekend with our three-year-old and drove to Spokane to meet S and the birth father. I proceeded for the next two and a half months to go to all of the doctor's appointments in Spokane. Every time I went, my dear friend Mandy flew with me. Her husband worked for Alaska Airlines at the time. She had free flights and we both flew for free. I was blessed to have her support.

Owen

Owen was due on August 27th but came early on August 21st. It was an entirely different experience. In the three years since Aidan had been born, the hospital had become more adoption friendly, and we had immediate access to him.

We were in the room for Owen's birth and Eric again cut the cord, but a nurse swept Owen out of the room immediately. He'd been born too cold on the Apgar scale and he was blue. (Apgar is a scoring system designed to quickly summarize the health of newborn children.)

A few minutes later, the nurse came back with the bundled-up baby in her arms and said, "Mom, take off your shirt." I looked at S and the nurse said, "No, Andrea. You're the Mom. Take off your shirt."

I removed my shirt and bra and the nurse nestled Owen in on me and wrapped both of us up in hot blankets. So there the three of us sat, with this new baby, and again, tears streaming down our faces. And I'm the Mom. It was such a powerful thing. Owen and I have a very, very strong bond.

And Eric and I have two beautiful sons.

Family of Choice

The boys do not have a relationship with S. We have an open adoption, but we had it in our written agreement that the only way she could spend time with either boy is if she's been clean for six months, and she's never been able to prove that.

When we adopted Owen, we almost didn't get him. The birth father changed his mind the night Owen was born and said "I'm not giving the baby up. I'll take care of him." He had neither a job, nor a place to live and a social worker got him to understand that if the baby didn't come to us, he would go into foster care. So, he did relinquish custody, but it was touch and go for six months. And he and S are no longer together.

Owen and S's second child have a full-sibling relationship and they're not in touch, but there are some things changing in that situation. As I write this, Aidan is 19, her first daughter is 18 and Owen is now 16.

A few years after Owen's birth, we got a call from the State of Washington asking us if we would be interested in a sibling placement. They said, "S had another baby almost a year ago, and she's been in foster care since the day she was born. She was born addicted to drugs." S was in jail at the time, and they'd found us through the court records. "You are a family placement. Are you interested in having the baby moved to you?"

We were stunned. We were like, "What!? What? A baby girl? Another child?"

I think Owen was five. We said yes. The state's caseworker, Corky, was amazing. She came and did a home study, and two weeks later, everything had been approved. Corky called me on a Monday said, "Prepare the nursery. We're coming on Saturday with the baby."

On Tuesday, I got another call from Corky letting us know that a family decision team meeting was scheduled for Thursday in downtown Seattle. Neither of us knew what to expect, but we showed up two days later.

Apparently, S had been released from jail—for dealing drugs—on that previous Tuesday afternoon. She was at the meeting and had brought her mom. S had burns up and down her arms (Meth? Heroin? I didn't know) and when I went to give her a great big hug, her mom stepped in between us. From behind her mom, S said, "You can have my boys, but you'll never get a hold of my girls."

Eric says we should have turned and left right then, but instead we all went into the meeting room. I've tried to block the whole experience because it was so horrific. I can't though, because it's burned into my memory. I even remember exactly what I was wearing that day.

It was awful to watch. Of course, the state wouldn't give S custody of the baby. So, her mom said, "My husband and I want custody." Her husband had been recently released from prison. The state would not place the baby with them.

Instead of giving the baby girl to us, S decided to leave the baby in the foster care system. We left, and Corky called me with updates every few weeks for several months. And then one day she called and said,

"Andrea, I'm retiring. Do you want to continue to get updates?"

By then I was done. It was painful, and I said, "I cannot think about this girl. I can't do it." Last I heard she was in Spokane. Every once in a while, I Facebook- and Instagram-stalk S just to see where she is and how they are all doing.

At one point, in between the boys, we were matched with another birth mother after the agency called us out of the blue. They said they had a mother who was due with a girl in December, and they couldn't find a family for her. The agency said, "She'd be perfect for your family" and then gave us a lot of reasons why. We told her we'd talk about it. We did and said yes. Two weeks later we got a call telling us the birth mother had been diagnosed bipolar, as was her mother. They advised us not to go through with the adoption and we walked away from that.

For many years, the thought of having our own child was still in my head. We went back to the same fertility clinic one more time. Things had changed and the doctor thought our odds of success were much higher.

And not surprisingly, the price was higher too, at $27K. We passed.

Back then, I thought that it was such a big fucking rip-off that I couldn't actually bear a child. I don't think that anymore, and I haven't in many years.

We Got Everything

I no longer feel like we got nothing. In reality, we got everything.

I am the mom of these two amazing kids, who I love with all my heart, beyond whatever capacity I once thought was possible. I have done a lot of self-work around it and I realize none of the shit matters. It doesn't matter if my kids came through me or to me. They're my heart. Our boys are our boys.

Our family is complete. Eric and I have two beautiful, wonderful, incredible sons.

From Mom to Mother

I was powerfully broken, powerfully defective, and powerless until I chose otherwise. As I said, my shit was warm and comfortable, and it took me some time to move out of it.

The minute I first held Aidan in my arms, I was like, "Oh my God, I'm his mom." And in that moment, it wasn't about me. It was about him. It was absolutely not about me and my experience getting there. It didn't fucking matter how I got there. What mattered was I was there, and I was a mom.

The same thing happened with Owen. He became mine when we sat skin-to-skin wrapped in hot blankets.

I remember the first time I felt like Aidan's mother. He must have been about six months old and, of course up until this moment, I'd been doing all the early mom things. Not sleeping, changing, feeding, burping, rocking—all the things. I'm not sure what it was about this particular moment that was so profound for me, and it doesn't matter.

We were in the car going somewhere and Aidan sneezed. I looked back at him in his car seat and snot was everywhere. I had nothing with which to clean him up. I pulled over, thinking, we can't go anywhere until I figure this out. I had a bunch of receipts in the car, and I used those to wipe up the snot, getting it all over me, but off of him. It was the first time I remember thinking: this is what a mom does. I wasn't just taking care of some other woman's child.

Maybe that's when I began to own all of it. I'm not sure. Those boys are mine. Acknowledging and allowing my own power in that is an ongoing gift to me. I am one thousand percent their mother.

Stronger on the Other Side of Broken

My experience with infertility and thinking of myself as broken and defective shows up in my life now as grace for other people. I don't know what other people are going through and it's not up to me to judge them. I didn't let a lot of people know what I was going through and it colored everything in my world.

It was hard for me to go to a baby shower; it was even difficult for me to go the grocery store sometimes and see moms and babies. I often felt judged along my infertility journey. I certainly constantly judged myself.

It was years after infertility before I overcame that. Years before I found my power in other ways. Eventually I found my voice and I was able to talk about that journey and those experiences without saying it was my fault.

I was all about resetting my expectations and being open to a new direction that I didn't expect, and frankly, couldn't even see. Now I can tell you definitively that this was the way we were meant to build a family.

As I said, I know now that I unintentionally chose—it was a choice, albeit unconscious—to think of myself as broken. As defective. As a victim of my circumstances.

I will tell you now that I am intentionally not broken. I am not fucking defective. I'm exactly who I'm supposed to be and how I'm supposed to be.

I'm grateful for my journey and so much stronger on this side of it.

Practice

Your Active Choice

Choose to Mend Your Broken

We all have some places in our lives that feel broken or defective. What does it look like for you to be responsible for your response to the experience?

Questions

- When and how have you felt broken in your life?
- Where in your life do you feel powerless?
- Have you created a victim mindset from your experience of broken? Are you choosing to stay in it rather than mend it? (That's a bonus question.)

- What have you gotten from your experience of feeling broken that you couldn't have gotten any other way?

Your 10-minute exercise:

Turn on some music (Alexa, play something I can dance to!) and get out of your head while you dance for 10 minutes.

Have extra time? Support your infertile sisters by getting to know their journey https://www.health.harvard.edu/newsletter_article/The-psychological-impact-of-infertility-and-its-treatment

Section 3: Unconscious

"I am not what happened to me. I am what I choose to become." – Carl Jung

When life throws you down – and it will – consider it a gift to get back up and face down the next challenge. You will turn dark into light. And I promise that, in hindsight, things will be the way they were meant to be. Realize that the only thing within your control is how you choose to react to something. Choose happiness, choose positivity, choose peace. You are enough.

The Other Side of Unconscious

I went back and forth about what I was going to call this section. I thought about calling it The Other Side of Death but that seemed kind of hyperbolic because I don't really remember feeling like I was going to die during this story I'm about to tell you. Eric thought I was going to die, though. In fact, he was told that I was dying, and he needed to say goodbye. Three times.

I'm clearly still alive. While we've established that I'm an intelligent woman, I don't actually know how to tell anyone to get to the stronger side of death. I have not yet been there and hope not to be for some time.

I was close to death, though. I just don't remember it. Because I was unconscious. In a coma.

So, as I wrote this, in reliving the experience, I decided to just call it like it was. In a lot of ways—as you'll see—I was fucking unconscious before my coma.

Hang on, because reading this section may be a bit of a bumpy ride. I'm just going to run through details and we'll get to the learning at the end. As you read, please give a shout out here and there to my patient, loving husband Eric. He has driven me to SO. MANY. HOSPITALS.

I Was Fat

By September of 2007, I felt like I *almost* had it all. I had a great business, an amazing family, the best husband, my favorite house at the beach (before the fire). I was in fairly good control (ha!) of everything in my life, but I couldn't control my weight.

It may not surprise you to know—and I'm just going to come right out and say it—that because of the way I grew up, and my learned and unexamined biases at the time, I believed that fat people were lazy, slovenly and stupid.

When I could not control my weight, I believed myself to be lazy, slovenly and stupid. I know it may not make conscious sense, but I'm being completely transparent here, and you know, the name of this section has unconscious in it. (I apologize now to everyone.)

Anyway. I decided to have lap band surgery. I had tried everything else to lose weight. Everything. All of the programs, all of the crazy diets, all of the things. I was still 220 pounds and I was miserable. I hated the summer because I was always hot and sweaty, and I felt disgusting.

I paid $15K for the elective surgery (cheaper than a kid through IVF!). Everything went fine and I began to lose weight. The lap band makes it harder to ingest food, so if you overeat, you throw up. I ended up losing a lot of weight fairly quickly.

Rah. Success.

In January, I had an ovarian cyst burst. It was the worst pain I'd ever felt in my life and beat out the tube-flushing experience during infertility treatments. The doctors said it looked like I had a few more cysts in my ovaries.

But I was still losing weight.

In February, another cyst burst while I was driving home from work. I drove myself to the Emergency Room and I can't believe I made it because, when I got there, my white blood count was low and the pain was worse than the first time. The ER doctor referred me to another doctor who said, "We need to remove that ovary."

I had an oophorectomy and a bonus appendectomy. The doctor said my appendix was inflamed and "standing up and waving at him," so it was going to have to come out anyway.

The next week, at my follow-up appointment, the doctor showed me photos of my uterus. He said, "This is the worst case of endometriosis I've ever seen in my entire career. And I see a lot." He's a teaching surgeon and was in the process of writing a textbook. He asked me to sign a release so he could use my uterus photos as examples of the worst endometriosis he'd ever seen.

I said, "Oh sure. Why not?" I'm pretty sure I rolled my eyes.

He also said my uterus needed to come out.

I said, "I need a second opinion." So, I went to a reproductive specialist, who confirmed the first opinion. I scheduled the hysterectomy for the end of April.

The second surgery was successful and left me with one ovary (which is now causing hot flashes as I near my fiftieth birthday, thank you very much).

Here comes the twist. I had both surgeries (the oophorectomy, the bonus appendectomy, and the hysterectomy) laparoscopically. They were done with a DaVinci robot, which was very forward technology at the time. During laparoscopy, the surgeon injects a carbon dioxide gas into the abdominal cavity to enhance visibility and accessibility. The doctors had no idea at the time that the procedure could tighten the lap band.

I kept going along just fine, though. I was still losing weight with the lap band, but I did notice that I could eat less and less before feeling ill.

Something's Wrong

At the very end of May on a Friday, Eric and I and the kids were driving from Snoqualmie to our beach house, and we stopped for dinner along the way.

I think I had a cup of soup. It was nothing big because I couldn't eat very much by then. After dinner, as we were driving, I kept feeling nauseated. Eric kept stopping the car so I could jump out and throw up. I was beginning to realize something was wrong, but I wasn't entirely sure what it was. Did it have to do with the lap band? Was it food poisoning? We continued to the beach house even though we must have stopped the car ten times during the two-and-a-half-hour drive.

By the middle of the night, I couldn't sleep. I couldn't walk. I couldn't talk. I was laying on the cold floor in the bathroom because every time I moved, I had to throw up. Eric called 911 and the ambulance came and took me to the community hospital in the little, tiny town near our beach house.

I told them everything I could about my situation, including that I had a lap band. They said I was dehydrated and had food poisoning, kept me overnight and sent me home with some pills.

Eric picked me up Saturday morning, and his mom came to pick up the kids so Eric could focus on me (which was a huge blessing, but we didn't know it at the time).

June 2008

At home, the feeling of being nauseated didn't stop. I kept throwing up and continued to feel worse. Eric called the doctors, who prescribed a suppository, which he drove back into town to pick up. That didn't work either. Eric bundled me in the car and drove me to Puyallup, two hours away, because he thought we'd have better luck there.

We made it to Puyallup's Good Samaritan hospital, where they told us there had been a six-car pileup on I-5 and probably a five-hour wait before somebody could see me. In the meantime, they put me on a blood pressure monitor because it kept dropping and was worrying to them.

It wasn't long before Eric literally said, "Fuck this," and got me back in the car and headed another 40 miles back to Snoqualmie Valley Hospital near where we lived. This was also the hospital that I drove myself to when I had the ovarian cyst. The doctor who diagnosed me was on duty. He took one look at me with my dropping blood pressure and said, "You have a problem we can't fix," called an ambulance, and sent me to Evergreen Hospital in Kirkland.

That was Sunday night, June 1. Around midnight, the doctor from the lap band clinic came in (not my doctor) and said, "We're going to go in and see what's going on." And that's all I remember for the next 17 days.

Truly Unconscious

E ric knew something was wrong because the surgery took much longer than the doctors had originally thought. They repaired a hole in my stomach about the size of a half dollar, and I aspirated on the table. The doctors thought I was probably aspirating before I even made it to the hospital. Fluid built up in my lungs. Less oxygen was reaching my bloodstream. I was intubated.

When I was back in a room in intensive care, hooked up to every Keep-Andrea-Alive machine imaginable, Eric overheard one of the nurses in the hallway say, "I hope she doesn't get ARDS." ARDS is an acronym for Acute Respiratory Distress Syndrome. Of course, Eric had no idea what that was or what it meant at the time. Most of us have heard of it now, because

ARDS is the primary cause of death among patients with COVID-19. At the time, it had a 70% mortality rate.

Within a day, I was diagnosed with ARDS. No one had any idea how long I'd been without oxygen, so I had lungs that didn't work and perhaps damage to my brain as well.

I was unconsciously uncooperative and aggravated by all the tubes and machines. I kept trying to take them out, to sit up. I tried to communicate in sign language because I was intubated and couldn't speak.

So, the doctors put me in a medical coma to shut me up and calm me down and ultimately to help me heal. I was unaware of any of this.

Eric, however, was not. He sat by my side, day after day and night after night, watching as a special bed was brought in. The new bed would turn my body so fluid buildup wouldn't hamper my progress. The bed rocked back and forth to stimulate circulation. He was there as I developed sepsis and an oozing rash from the middle of my back down to the back of my knees. He was there for three blood transfusions.

Eric was the one sitting there each time (at least three) the doctors told him I wouldn't make it through the day. Or the night. And that he needed to prepare for the worst.

I did not spend a night in the hospital alone. Eric was there for all but two nights, when my Dad filled in.

Eric is a very private person who doesn't tell his business to the world like his wife does, but I think it's important to share this so others can understand what he experienced and how he was able to do what he did.

He hadn't been home for a few days on the day I was intubated, so my dad came to stay with me, and Eric went home to see the boys and shower. He said, "I was in the shower, crying my eyes out, and I just sank to the floor and told myself that this is not in my control. I will just be there for Andrea and do whatever I need to do to help get us through this." He told me from that point on, he didn't look anything up, he didn't want to know about ARDS. He said he didn't want to know statistics, he just wanted to focus on me getting better.

Eric was able to sneak the boys in one day and told me a story about Aidan, who was six at the time (Owen was three) standing on a chair next to my bed, dressed in scrubs and a mask, waving his arms over me like an orchestra conductor, saying, "Breathe, Mommy! One, two, three. Breathe!"

I Woke Up

Seventeen days after the surgery, I woke up. I recall a moment when I turned to Eric, who was sitting on a chair next to me and said, "Hey do you have my cell phone?" He just slumped over and started crying. That question made him realize my brain was functioning.

I remember talking to the doctor about this later, and he said, "Yeah, you did that. We were shocked and in awe and amazed at your spirit, that you were able to do that." He told me that they asked me a series of questions when I woke up. I told them I thought it was June 1st or 2nd, and that I was at Swedish Hospital in Seattle. I was wrong on both answers.

I don't remember much of anything from my coma. But I woke up with songs playing in my head. It finally dawned on me to ask Eric about it. "Did you sing to me?" Eric said, "Every single day."

For days and weeks and months after my coma, I would hear songs in my head. I'd ask Eric about a Commodores song or a Kenny Rogers song or some other random tune I hadn't heard in ten years, and he'd say, "Yes, I sang that, too." Eric's voice is a gift. He is an amazing singer and he shared that gift with me.

I do recall some fascinating dreams, and I've dreamt them periodically since, which I also find strange. They are still very clear to me 12 years later. There was one dream where I was on a helicopter landing pad and I was absolutely freezing. I was sitting in the middle of the landing pad and the helicopter was coming in and I couldn't move. In another dream I had my baby in a stroller and we were in a maze that was so dark I couldn't see, but I knew I had to make it through the maze. We kept bumping into walls and going down dead-ends. The weirdest dream happened at an amusement park, and I was on the Zipper ride (which goes upside down). I had endless change falling out of my pockets and I felt like I was never getting off the ride. They wouldn't stop for me, but they stopped and let everyone else off.

When I talked to the doctor about the dreams, he said, "You were on a selection of drugs that could have done anything to your brain."

Home

I stayed in the ICU for a couple of days and then moved to a step-down floor. I was so thirsty, but it was too soon for me to drink water, so I conned one of the night nurse's helpers into giving me ice chips. She got in trouble the next day. Eric said, "Andrea, you can't do that." And I said, "But I was so thirsty! I asked for ice, I didn't ask for water."

I was already pushing the boundaries and ready to control my way out of that hospital. (Remember, I didn't learn the lesson about control until after the fire.)

Once I woke up and started on the road to recovery, our insurance carriers began threatening not to pay the hospital bill. Eric was in human resources for the Seattle Seahawks, where he still works, and was aware of what was happening behind the scenes. So, he was watching it.

The hospital was telling us I needed to be there longer because I hadn't recovered enough to go to a rehab program. My muscles had atrophied so much I couldn't walk. I pushed for release for five days after I woke up. I think it was five days total when we realized the insurance wasn't going to be paying that bill.

I won't go into the details, but we're still paying. It was reduced from the original $1.2M to $800K and we've got it down to $80K now.

Anyway, we had two choices. I could stay in the hospital and we'd pay out of pocket, or I could go home. Eric decided we'd go home, with the understanding that I needed two weeks of 24-hour care and that we'd stay in contact with the doctors at Evergreen.

I went home, and had babysitters morning, noon and night. Eric had to carry me up and down the stairs. So many people helped. They sat with me, they helped with the boys, they cooked for us, they took care of us. I'm so grateful for those people in my life.

The week after I got out of the hospital, Aidan turned seven. I had started planning his birthday party before the coma. Unbeknownst to me, my two amazing friends, Mandy and Kelly, took over and pulled off the party, including gifts from me and Eric and showing up in a wheelchair accessible van to get me to the party. I'm in tears now as I remember it. I wasn't able to do much, but I was there.

Recovery

It took me a long time to recover. It was over a month before I could get out of the wheelchair. And then I used a walker for another six weeks. I fought exhaustion every day for five or six months. I finally tried to start going back to work in October (more than a year after my lap band surgery) for half-days. I could only do two hours. I think I made it back to work for half-days in January.

You know how I did it? I controlled everything I could control. I was able to move forward by saying, "Ok. One foot in front of the other. I'm getting rid of this wheelchair by this date. I'm getting rid of this walker by this date, I'm going to have enough stamina to be at my desk for four hours by this date." I set goals. I didn't always make them, but I set them and worked toward them.

The first time I went to rehab, the woman who checked me in said, "Where's your oxygen tank?" I didn't have one. She said, "I've never met anybody who has had ARDS that hasn't come out without needing supplemental oxygen." I was grounded from flying for two years. And when I did finally fly, I had to make sure they had oxygen tanks on board. The only thing I experience now that I didn't before is altitude sickness and a massive headache when I fly. It's all because of the damage to my lungs.

It was the next spring before I really felt like me again. I had gotten stronger doing some rehab, but insurance only paid for ten appointments. When they cut me off, my rehab specialist, a woman named Candy, said, "You are not ready. I want you to start Pilates twice a week," and she gave me a referral to a Pilates instructor—Jana Broecking—who is now one of my dearest friends.

Jana got me back to being balanced and strong. I realized then—and it's been a long wake-up call that's still happening—that being physically strong and physically able is much more important to me than my weight.

Owning It

It took me eight or nine years to actually talk about my coma, particularly in public. I didn't want to admit my part in it, and it's my story. I'm very comfortable admitting it now, but it took the instigation of sharing it fully to start moving forward with it.

I sat on an executive board with the CEO of Evergreen Hospital, and we got to talking. I said, "Hey, I need to thank you and your staff for saving my life." And he said, "Will you give a speech at an upcoming event for us?" I was like, "No way, I'm not talking about this. It was a long time ago and people don't want to hear it."

It took him about three weeks to convince me that I could stand up in front of a large gathering of staff members and their spouses as the "Patient Success Story." I think it was his belief that "they need to hear it" that worked. So, I wrote a speech and practiced it to death. I don't usually practice my speeches much, but I practiced and practiced because I was so nervous about it.

It took me back there, to all of that, and it was hard. But once I did it I could do it again and do it again because I need to own my own part in that story. There's a reason I got ill. And part of it was my own decision to not be fat.

Stronger on the Other Side of Unconscious

A s I said at the beginning of this section, in a lot of ways I was unconscious before my coma. I'm still learning from it.

My husband and I have a very good relationship. We've been together for 28 years and I adore the man. All along, we've had this relationship where I just take the reins. It's who I am. I just take the reins, and I go, and it works for us. His strength is in his complete support and love.

When I came out of my coma, Eric had to take the reins on everything. And for a while I had to let him, and it was fucking miserably hard for me. I wanted to say, "No, do it this way. My way is better." Sound familiar? I got kicked out of Girl Scouts for it.

Eric was doing his damnedest to get me back to healthy, and he was doing it the only way he knew how. So, I had to let him do it and that was an incredible lesson for me in letting go, which is not something I was ever good at. I believed if something was going to get done "right," I was going to do it myself.

I know now how wrong I was. Every time I did that, I denied him his right to care for me.

My coma changed the dynamic of our marriage in a very positive way. Change is always hard. Change is always, "Oh shit, how are we going to come out stronger on the other side of this?"

Conscious at Home

My coma experience literally and metaphorically woke me up. It flipped a switch and made my life better. I became conscious to so much that I had been unaware of before it happened. It caused me to change my perspective on what is important in life.

Years ago, I hosted a radio show, Artful Moxie, and during an episode, I said on air that the coma was one of the best things that ever happened to me. I came home from that show, and Eric said, "Don't you ever say that again. It was the worst part of my life. You weren't there, you don't have any idea what it felt like." And he's right. I don't. I wasn't there. He was, and we have two distinct experiences of that time.

Knowing now that the only thing I control is my response to everything that happens to me, I choose to see the coma as perfect for me. I learned to be a better partner, a better parent, and a better leader because of the coma. I'm a better human, really.

I'm so much more appreciative of my family now. I'm more grateful for the time I get to spend with them. I'm more aware of that time because I realize how fleeting it is. There are times when I understand to my core that I am living on borrowed time. I have been given another chance—not to do things right, but to do things differently.

When I was living unconsciously, I was so concerned with my own voice—that voice that I fought so hard to have. I was demanding and argumentative. I wasn't open to new experiences or going with the flow. And now I really am. I'd rather just be than schedule every minute of every day.

I think I was so concerned with getting things done and being in charge. I liked being in control of every little thing, even my kids. Now I'd rather find out from my kids what they want to do and then do that. I don't need to tell them what I think they should do. I'm better at helping them solve issues because I'm not telling them what to do.

In hindsight, I look at the way I parented my oldest until he was seven (before the coma) and I was so controlling. I felt any "wrong" behavior reflected on me. He's a brilliant, smart, funny, intelligent kid. Why couldn't I just let him be that? Now I'm conscious of all of that. I don't know if I succeed all the time because I don't think anybody does, honestly, but I am aware of it.

Conscious at Work

At my company, I was a controlling micromanager before the coma. I was of the mind that nobody could do things as fast or efficiently or as creatively or as well as I, and again, I was dead wrong.

I was away from Artitudes for eight months, and the company had to run. Eric, my brother-in-law, my business coach Ron, and a couple guys from my Vistage group who are still lifelong friends stepped in to help run my company. (I laugh because it makes me feel awfully good that it needed ALL of those men versus me to get it done.)

What happened while I was gone is that people did what they were supposed to do. They did what they were trained to do, and they did it without me standing over their shoulders and questioning it or trying to push my way into their stuff.

After my coma, I was able to say, "Hey, this company still ran, these people are good at what they do. I don't have to reengage in all of these things. Because I wasn't able to do it, they all stepped up and did what they needed to do. When I came back, I realized I didn't have to do all of that. I didn't have to work myself to death anymore."

I got out of their faces. I got out of their way, and I got out of my own way. And we flourished.

Conscious in Life

Every year I get a little of what I think is PTSD in June, around the time of my coma, and 2020 was particularly hard because a lot of the people dying of COVID-19 have died from ARDS. It's been devastating to watch in a lot of ways. I know how hard it was for my family and so I feel deeply for the people who love those who are going through what I did.

Brutal isn't even a big enough word for it. I've never been able to find the words to express the way I feel or to express my devastation and my dismay at what's going on for those patients and families.

I've always been an empathetic person to some degree. It comes naturally for me to feel others' pain and relate to where they are.

The coma shifted that for me because I became able to see more sides of the coin. There aren't two sides to every coin. There are about 27 sides to every coin. What I know now is that if you have very distinct ideas about how something should be or how something is, then you're never open to learning about what could be or what somebody else's experience is, and it's almost impossible to put yourself in someone else's shoes.

Being conscious enables me to be more empathetic, and maybe not put myself in their shoes, but put myself beside them or behind them so that I can learn from them.

Practice

Your Active Choice

Choose to Awaken Your Unconscious

What does it look like for you to wake up to those places you are unaware of creating? How can you be responsible for your response to the experience?

Questions

- What do you not accept about yourself?
- Where in your life are you unconscious?
- Have you created a victim mindset around whatever it is you don't like about yourself? Are you willing to put yourself in harm's way to change the thing you don't like? (That's a bonus question.)

- What have you gotten from your experience of being unconscious that you couldn't have gotten any other way?

Your 10-minute exercise:

Spend 10 minutes writing a list of everything you're grateful for about yourself and your life. Include the people you count on to drive you to the hospital.

Have extra time? Breathe.

https://www.health.harvard.edu/mind-and-mood/relaxation-techniques-breath-control-helps-quell-errant-stress-response

Section 4: Fire

"She wore her scars as her best attire. A stunning dress made of hellfire." – Daniel Saint

Things don't always have to be hard. You do not always have to prove yourself. No matter how terrible things seem, it won't be the end of everything. There's always a new day, a new chapter, the turn of a page. You are enough.

The Other Side of Fire

Recently Eric and I were walking along the beach, talking about our ups and downs, highs and lows, what we're dealing with right now, and he said, "I feel like our marriage has been forged in fire."

Glancing at our beach house in the distance, I said, "Quite literally, sweetheart."

My Relationship with Fire

T hings are frequently on fire in my world. My birth sign is Aries, which is a fire sign, and I'm also Aries rising, so you could say I'm double fire. At one time, I thought a house fire was something distant, a story that you hear about in a book or on the news. Most of us think, "Oh, that will never affect my life. It's not that common anymore."

Well, my life has been affected by fire five times.

We bought the beach house in 2006. On our first Fourth of July there, a rogue firework started a fire in the dunes. We have a little over a third of a mile of protected sand dunes that grow between us and the sea. If you were to stand on our deck and look straight out at the ocean, you'd see a green expanse all the way out to the water. On that day, the dunes caught fire and the flames started coming towards us at a fairly rapid rate. The fire department had to come in and put them out. But it was scary for all of us.

The Fourth of July causes some anxiety every year.

A few years later the boys and I wound up on the news after we watched a crazy person drive up on the beach approach (which is not a road) and get his vehicle stuck when he high-centered on the dunes. It set them on fire. We were just out for a walk. The guy had an extra gas tank in his car, and it caught fire and burned 30 acres. That fire also came toward the house, and the fire department put it out. Again.

A few years after that, on August 4, 2014, the beach house caught fire, which you already know about if you read the introduction. If you didn't read it (some people go right to Chapter 1) I highly recommend it.

Then, on that same date a few years later, my neighbor across the street from our Snoqualmie house was terribly injured when his house caught fire and burned after his compost bin self-combusted. Ten months later when his house was about halfway rebuilt—they'd just put the windows in—some rags ignited in the garage, started a huge blaze, and the newly rebuilt house burnt to the ground.

I have a relationship with fire. And while I wouldn't have said this even three years ago, it's become a healthy, respectful relationship. As I said in the introduction, fire gave me one of the biggest gifts in my life—the deep-down certainty that I am not in control of anything. The coma started me on the path to that understanding. The fire burned away the last of my resistance to it.

August 4th, 2014

T he boys and I had just started our annual month-long stay at the beach house. This was back before they were teenagers and young adults with their own lives who say things like, "Nope, not spending a month with mom in a remote place. Sorry." But back then they loved it, or at least didn't know better.

We'd play on the beach all day. Our goal was always challenging ourselves to see how long we could go without getting in the car for anything. The house is about three miles from town. We rode bikes to get groceries and would do whatever we could to not get in the car, and that meant walking, swimming, biking, horseback riding. It was always my favorite month of the year.

At the beach house, I got to spend time with my family in a way that was not pressured by outside influences like work or school or even other people. It was my haven, my little castle.

August 4th had been a beautiful sunny day of bike riding and playing at the beach. We had eaten dinner and decided to take a meander down the road and back. I was walking. Aidan, 13, and Owen, almost 10, were riding their bikes. As you know, because you read the Introduction, while we were walking, the fog rolled in. We were in shorts, and it was quickly damp and cold. The boys and I hurried our way back to the house and I put a Duraflame® log on to warm it up.

By this time, I think it was about eight o'clock, but I don't remember the exact time. I asked the kids to brush their teeth, we did the bedtime stuff, and I sent them up to bed.

I was relaxing, warm and cozy with the fire burning nicely. About 20 minutes after the boys were in bed, I heard a noise that sounded like a jet airplane landing on my roof, and it freaked me out. I went running outside to look for the cause of the noise. I was standing on the back deck looking up when I heard somebody honking their horn in my driveway. That in itself was weird because I hadn't closed the gates and I usually did that right after the kids went to bed. Eric was in Seattle and I didn't expect him home that night.

So, I poked my head over the side of the house from the back deck and the guy honking his horn saw me and yelled, "You have a chimney fire!" He said there were sparks coming from the chimney. I ran inside and I got a pitcher full of water and put out the fire in the fireplace.

Then I walked outside, down the stairs and out on the trail far enough that I could see the roof on our three-story house. Everything looked fine. I walked around the house and back inside and I saw no sparks, no fire and nothing else going on.

I'd tried calling Eric and he wasn't picking up. He was playing poker with his best friend Toby, who is married to my friend Mandy. So, I called Mandy and asked her to have Eric call me.

Eric called and asked me to go back out and look again while we were on the phone. I walked on to the deck and didn't see anything. I went out front. "Everything's fine," I told Eric. He said, "Walk down the trail."

When I walked down the trail again, I saw flames on the roof near the chimney on the back side of the house. From where I was standing the fire did not look very big, maybe like the size of a dinner platter. But it was big enough to make me say "Oh shit, really?" My brain went into emergency mode and I said, "Eric, I've got to go, the roof is on fire!"

I was calling 911 as I was running up the stairs to the kids' room. They were in bunk beds (there were three sets in their room) and they liked the top, so each of them was on the top bunk.

Aidan sleeps like a freaking log, so he was out. Owen said, "Hi, Mommy," because he was still awake ninety minutes after going to bed. I started yelling, "UP! UP! Clothes on, get outside! The roof is on fire!" while I was still on the phone with 911.

The first fire truck showed up seven or eight minutes after I called them. The boys and I were outside standing in the driveway. I had moved my car—my favorite-ever Audi convertible—to a neighbor's driveway.

In that time, I had gone back upstairs, grabbed a bag that I thought had my tennis shoes in it (I later learned it was my work laptop; they were in similar bags) and threw it in the trunk of my car before I moved it.

Aidan and Owen came down the stairs and Aidan was in underwear, flip flops and a zip up fleece. I looked at him, looked at the roof and said, "Let's go, we're going back in and getting you clothes, because we don't know when we'll get back in." He tells the story to this day that I sent him into a burning house.

The fire trucks arrived, took out the gate that was cemented into the ground, and threw it into the empty lot next door so they could bring in the ladder truck.

Our beautiful house, that looks a Cape Cod up on stilts, became a five-alarm fire that blocked our street at both ends and required three different fire departments. Within about 30 minutes after I talked to Eric, the entire roof was up in flames, and the fire was in the walls. We learned you could hear the smoke alarms going from half a mile away because every smoke alarm in the house was screaming, and I found out the next day that a couple of them had melted and slid down the walls.

The boys and I stood in the neighbor's driveway and watched the house burn while we cried. Nobody questioned who we were; all of the police and fire fighters assumed we were neighbors. Finally, the police chief came by in his SUV, rolled down his window and called out, "Are you the homeowner?" I nodded. He said, "We didn't know you were here. Get in my car, you must be freezing."

He asked if we had anywhere we could go. We didn't. We couldn't leave because the streets were blocked, and I didn't have my purse. I realized later I had actually locked my purse in the trunk of my car with my work bag. To this day I don't remember doing it.

The fire chief called his nephew, who worked at a hotel in town, and explained the situation. He said, "We have a room for them. Just bring them here and we won't worry about payment tonight."

And that's where we were at midnight when Eric made it to us from Seattle. We were alive, smelling like smoke on what felt like a cellular level, and too jacked up to sleep.

The Aftermath

Sometime during the night when I wasn't sleeping, I posted on Facebook. I was in the middle of a daily gratitude challenge, so I posted that I was grateful for fast responses, smoke alarms, people who cared and being alive. Of course, my phone started blowing up.

Around 5:40 a.m. I was sitting at the Shiloh Inn looking out at the ocean and my friend Kelly called. She said, "We left the house ten minutes ago and we'll be there as soon as we can. What do you need?" I told her that we were okay, and they didn't need to come. She blew me off and said, "We're already on our way, don't even tell me not to come."

Before long Kelly and her husband Quinn met us at the hotel with essential toiletries and clothes and bags of stuff for the boys. I had everything except a bra.

Walmart doesn't carry 34G (which stands for "Geez, are you kidding me?").

We went to the beach house and met in the driveway with the fire and police departments; everything was cordoned off with yellow caution tape. Even though I'd stood and watched it burn, something in me had held out hope that we'd be back in the house the next day. But when I walked up to the house, I knew there was no going back.

The fire officials said not to go in, and the police said not to go in. As soon as they all left, Eric said, "Well, I'm going in." So, he did, along with Quinn, who was Navy Special Forces or something super cool like that. It was far worse than they expected. The top floor had burned completely, and some of the second floor, too. Water and smoke damage ruined everything else. There wasn't much to salvage. The boys were upset about losing their brand-new iPads.

A short while later, Quinn came out of the house like a conqueror holding two iPads up in the air. He had found them on an end table by the couch. Apparently, a piece of the ceiling had fallen down and covered them up. The boys went crazy, screaming "Quinn's our hero!" It was a bright spot on a smoky morning.

We really started rebuilding that morning. Within a couple of hours, the insurance agents appeared (I had called them at 6:00 a.m.). They brought us a check for $10K so that we could buy essentials and pay for a place to stay. People rallied around us in the most amazing way.

A neighbor we didn't know came by and told Kelly he was a former fire marshal for the city of Everett and that he had been at the scene the night before but had not realized we were there. He said we were welcome to stay in his guest house. If he'd known we were there he would have bundled us up and taken us there last night. Bruce Hansen and his wife Beckie are now some of our dearest friends.

The next morning, I called Al, the neighbor who owned the house where I'd parked my Audi, and he said he had a house for sale on the other side of Ocean Shores. We were welcome to use it even though it was being shown frequently. He'd call the real estate agent and get the keys for us.

At the hotel before we left that morning, we'd randomly run into an acquaintance named Mike (it's a small town), who told us his best friend was a master builder in town and offered to call him to come take a look at the house. So, while we went to meet the police, Mike called his friend Pat. Pat showed up in our driveway right after the police left and told us he'd always wanted to see the inside of our house.

He, too, pretended not to see the caution tape, went in to take a look and said, "I don't have any time at all, but I want this project. I'll rebuild this house for you."

Obviously, we didn't hire him that day, but everything was falling into place while the house was basically still hot. After Pat left, I called Al's real estate agent to talk about getting the keys to his place and she said, "Oh, Hi, Andrea! I heard you just met with my father-in-law Pat Brunstad."

In less than a day we'd had two offers for housing, a check from the insurance company, a builder and the boy's iPads.

Did I mention that the roof had fallen in on the beds where the boys had been sleeping? Yeah, we'd lost our house, but we hadn't lost any of us.

And as I mentioned in the Introduction, through fire I lost myself, and found myself. Turns out the fire wasn't really out yet (metaphorically). I still had some hot coals to walk through. And some control issues to examine.

Controlling the Narrative

The ease of everything falling into place on that first day didn't last. On the night of the fire when I was on the phone with Eric, I was thinking, "Maybe it's not too bad. We might be back in tomorrow." I did that because I wanted to control the situation. And also, in that case, because I wanted to control my emotions. I had to be the strength for my family. Eric was up in Seattle. I was there with my boys and I had to be strong for them.

So, my narrative that night was, "Everything's okay, we're fine. We'll go back to the house tomorrow and see what's going on. We're all good, guys. We'll go sleep in a hotel tonight. It'll be an adventure."

I was controlling the narrative to control my emotions. Because the truth was, I was utterly devastated. I felt like a piece of myself burnt up in that fire and I was never getting that piece back.

I held onto that control with the iron grip of desperation, rarely letting my guard down or my feelings out.

One day about a week after the fire I allowed myself to feel some of my pain and grief about the house. The insurance company wanted to come and catalog the house. I called Mandy to vent because I knew how hard it was going to be. I said, "I have to do this tomorrow and I'm just dreading it." And then I sat on the couch in our neighbor's house and cried. It was the day Robin Williams died. Aidan asked if I was okay. I said, "No, I'm just not." He sat on the couch with me, and we watched child appropriate Robin Williams videos while I cried. It helped a little.

Cataloging the House

T he next day was gray and rainy as happens on the
coast and the kids and I were getting ready to go
to the house. I had nowhere for the kids to go so
planned to let them stay mostly in the car with their
iPads while I worked with the insurance people.

And then Mandy, the angel, showed up on my
doorstep and said, "Alright boys, what movie are we
going to see?" I had never been so grateful to see my
friend in my life. She's there for every important thing
in my life—bad and good. She put her life on hold and
took care of the boys while I had the horrendous task of
cataloging the house. It took us three days. She stayed
the whole time. She put her life on pause, brought her
daughter down and entertained my boys.

Two adjusters and I set about cataloging our stuff.
Half of it was gone, so I had to go from memory and

guess what was in each room. It was incredibly hard. The kitchen was intact, so that was easy. Half of the master bedroom was gone. The only part that still stood was an alcove with the bed in it and the bed was fine. I had bought a really cool bright orange patterned quilt for our bed about two weeks before the fire and I was able to save it. In fact, I built the colors of the new master around that quilt. So, there were little bright spots, reminders that it could have been so much worse.

We couldn't catalog the boys' room at all because the roof had fallen in on it, on their beds, a reminder that my kids could have died, that if things had gone differently, they wouldn't be here.

I was happy when those three days were over. I've always said I'd never wish infertility on anybody. I'd never wish that cataloging experience on anyone, either.

It was absolutely horrible.

Rebuilding

When I went inside the house that first day (I also ignored the yellow tape) and saw the devastation, the damage, I knew that we weren't getting back in. I knew that we wouldn't be able to save the house.

After talking with a couple of other builders, we ended up hiring Pat, the man who came to the house that first morning. He was not the cheapest, but he knew how to work with insurance and every house he built was simply stunning.

My way of controlling the situation, just as with coming back from the coma, was one step forward, one step forward, one step forward. Pat first told us he'd have us back in the house in six months. It took nearly a year, and I was angry and bitter about it. This time we had great insurance, but horrible, horrible mortgage banks who wouldn't release funds to the builder, so he would stop working until the funds were released. It was a year-long battle.

When I was rebuilding myself after the coma, I controlled by setting goals. But with the rebuilding of the house, I didn't control anything. I had no say in when they put the roof on. I couldn't control when the drywall was going up or how long it took for the electrical permits or inspections to be passed. There were a lot of tears and a lot of me trying to control a situation I couldn't. I did realize—at the very least—that it wasn't doing any of us any good.

I Missed My House

I had a lot of deep, dark nights. Eric and I don't fight or argue a whole heck of a lot but he was not happy with the way I reacted to losing and rebuilding the house. I remember telling him that it was the hardest thing I've ever been through. And he responded, "What? The coma wasn't?" And I said, "Baby, I wasn't there for the coma. You were."

And in the same way, I said to him about the house "You weren't there. You were not there as we stood across the street and watched the house burn down." I don't want to diminish his experience because the place is a part of him as well, but he wasn't attached in the same way.

I missed my house. I missed me. I missed the Andrea I was when I was there. I missed the outlet of the beach. I truly believe the air is different. It's more oxygenated. I feel mentally and physically healthier there. I think I'm the best version of myself there. I felt like my heart had been ripped out.

The fire was a loss of what I held most dear about myself. I had given the beach house the status of being the only place in the world I could really truly be me. It's not true, of course, but that's how I felt at the time and periodically it's how I feel now. I feel content there.

The day that it hit me the hardest, and the day that I felt the most grief, was actually at the end of December. We'd been staying at a community up the coast, and it had been nearly five months since the fire. We had a new puppy named Lola, and my beloved Grandma Gerry had just died. It was a gray, rainy, wet, nasty day. We went down to the house because we wanted to see the progress and learned there was no progress. There were no walls. There were no floors. It was all two-by-fours and water was pouring in through the roof.

I sat down on the wet floor with the rain soaking into me and cried my eyes out. That's when the bottom dropped out. I had cried before, I had talked about it, but I hadn't really felt it. That was the day I began to let the emotion out. It was another one of those moments I'll remember forever. It's the day I began the healing process.

That doesn't mean I didn't try to control it. In fact, I was so annoyed with how long it was taking, as the rebuild continued, I told everybody on Facebook how unhappy I was with Pat. In fact, I said, "Its's April and my house is still not done. It was supposed to be done in six months. And then February and then he said March. And here it is almost May and my house is still not done." He was pissed. And I don't blame him. We have since mended that fence and it took both of us to get there.

Pat is a terrific builder. The beach house is our home, and it looks like something you'd find in a magazine. But more importantly, it feels like us. And we now have a gas fireplace and a metal roof. And more peace of mind.

Stronger on the Other Side of Fire

That day in December was when I began to move to the stronger side of the experience. Until then, I hadn't been able to feel the emotion quite as deeply as I did that day. It was something about the atmosphere, as well, and grief about losing my grandmother that created the perfect storm.

What I learned through the process of the fires is that there's so much that's not in my control, whether I want it in my control or not. It's a total illusion to say that I have control of any situation. And that was not something I had really been able to name before, even through the infertility treatments where I was out of control, even through my coma where I was completely out of control.

There's also a lesson for me about owning my part in my own experience. I could easily say this happened to me or this happened to us. And I don't like to look at it that way necessarily. I'd rather say, yes, we had a fire. I mean, I'm sure there are things we could have done differently. We'd had the chimney cleaned three years before, but maybe we needed it cleaned more often. Maybe I should have called 911 sooner. I don't want to blame us, but I also don't want to not take the blame if that makes any sort of sense.

Like I've said previously, suffering happens. It's not like I set my own house on fire. I didn't do that. But what came from it was my doing and I struggled mightily with not getting the house rebuilt fast enough. I was depressed. I was sad. I lashed out at the builder. I felt like a victim in my own story, telling myself that the only place in the world I could be myself was gone. That's not true. I can be myself anywhere I want.

What I really am aware of in my life is not saying something happened to me. Yes, this happened. I can't control it, but I can control my response.

At this moment, I am grateful for my relationship with fire. I am certain there will be other times in my life when something goes up in flames, and I hope it's metaphorically, but I know I can't control it.

I'm standing right now at the picture window in the living room, looking at the gorgeous blue sea and sky. I feel at peace. I give myself permission to be me. Wherever I am.

Practice

Your Active Choice

Choose to Embrace Your Fires

We all have shit burning in our lives. What does it look like for you to be responsible for your response to the things on fire in your life?

Questions

- What's your version of fires burning in your world?
- What stories are you telling yourself about control?
- Have you created a victim mindset from your experience of trying to control your world? Where in your life are you out of control? (That's a bonus question.)

- What have you gotten from your experience of trying to control something that you couldn't have gotten any other way?

Your 10-minute exercise:

Take 10 minutes and jot down a quick letter to someone you've yelled at when you felt out of control. Feel free to address it to Pat. You don't have to give it to anyone. This is for you.

Have extra time? Surrender.

https://thriveglobal.com/stories/the-art-of-surrendering-learning-how-to-let-go-of-control/

Section 5: It's Okay to be Sad

"Something that is loved is never lost."
– Toni Morrison

Own your own path. You'll hear so many voices telling you who you should be, what you should be doing. But embrace each moment as your own. Things will change. Change is constant. Your life will change, your friendships will change, your circumstances will change. So, live each moment and breathe each breath. Don't wish away today because the path will wind away from this moment and onto the next and what seemed to loom so large will look so small in the rear-view mirror. You are enough.

The Other Side of Grief

A business coach once told me I was too happy—surprising now that you know about my childhood and early years, huh? I think it's a fair assessment for someone who doesn't know my story. It's not true, but it's fair.

The truth is that if you give me a happiness scale today of 1-10 and I say I'm a six, somebody's dead. Because my happiness scale is different than most people.

Of course, I asked my business coach to tell me more and she said, "I think you're inauthentic because you don't feel sad. Ever." Please imagine an entire line of the "rolling on the floor laughing" emoji here.

The truth is I'm happy because I've learned to be. I choose happy. There are times when I can't, sure, but most of the time, I'm actively choosing happy.

I said to my business coach, "I do feel sad. I recognize it. I acknowledge it. I realize it's there. When my Grandma Gerry died in 2014, I was devastated. I was sad for a long time. I cried often then, and I still cry periodically when I think about her."

What I didn't say is that for a long time I was sad about a being a girl. That my heart broke into pieces every time an IUI didn't make a baby, and that I grieved every child that almost came to me, natural or adopted. What I didn't say is that I don't watch the news because part of me hurts every time I hear about a family losing a loved one to COVID-19 and ARDS. What I didn't say is that I will never hear about a fire without feeling some level of fear and empathy for those involved.

We tend to think of grief specifically in relationship with death. My life has shown me that grief exists in all my losses, and that it's an insightful teacher that demands learning.

Grief from Death

Learning about life from death is an opportunity I think many of us run from rather than move toward. We'd rather escape it. As I get older, I see all grief as a gift I can invite in, hang out with, and tap into for celebration and connection. I don't have a huge amount of experience with it, yet it's already taught me much, and it continues to show up and ask for my attention.

Someone recently asked me, "Andrea, what's the value of grief for you?" In that moment, I struggled a bit with the answer, because my brother-in-law was just diagnosed with advanced cancer and I was seeing grief through the lens of his possible death. I said something like this, "The value of grief is a hard one to address right now because I'm grieving my brother-in-law even though he's still here. I'm not seeing value in today, although it's making me appreciate who he is."

We live our lives going along day by day, and while I don't want to say I take people for granted, I do think I have a tendency to not really appreciate the part people play in my life until I'm grieving them.

The value of grief for me (when it comes to my dead people), is that it's an appreciation of who they are and who they helped me become. Grief gives me an introspective lens to see how I was changed by knowing them. Those I have loved and lost have changed me immeasurably and I'm committed to celebrating them and keeping them alive in the world.

When we are open to seeing them, grief gives us gifts that are not available to us in any other way.

Joy from Grief

Every time I bake something from scratch without a recipe, I'm celebrating my Grandma T, who died three weeks before I turned 14 in 1985. From the time I was a young child, I got to spend a week on my own every summer with her and my grandpa, and I would be at their house every chance I got. I was very close to both of my grandparents.

My Grandma T died of a heart attack when she was gardening in her backyard. My Grandpa T was out there with her, but she was gone by the time he got to her. She was only in her sixties, and it was devastating to lose her. I remember crying for weeks. I just couldn't believe she was there one minute and gone the next. That was the hardest thing for me at that age. There was absolutely no warning.

Grandma T was my first significant death and I still remember her funeral quite clearly. It was open casket, and I remember how brutal that was. She looked like her, but she was still and pale, and my grandmother was never still and never pale. I remember not wanting to go up to the casket, and my mom holding my hand when I did. Grandma T's was the first funeral I'd attended, and it was hard. I think you get better at those things as you have more experience, but it's never easy, especially when it's somebody you love so much.

Grandma T, even after 35 plus years without her, still comforts me with the love she showered on me through cooking. She was highly creative in the kitchen. I remember one year I called her and I said, "Grandma, I want to make Christmas gifts for people, and I want to make food." And she said, "Okay, we'll have your parents drop you off this weekend."

We spent an entire weekend in December baking cookies and fudge. She taught me how to do everything without recipes. I hold all of that very dear because I find a lot of joy in baking and cooking. It's how I relax.

I wouldn't be who I am without her, and neither would my family. Her love lives on through me in the very tangible taste and comfort of the dishes I cook for my loved ones.

Grandma T was my safe place, and the place I always wanted to be. I still miss her.

Hope from Grief

G randpa T lived until March of 2000. Eric and I would go to breakfast or lunch with him at least once a month and grandpa always ordered chicken fried steak, no matter what time of day it was. I adored him. I wrote poetry about him in high school, and he taught me the two-step shuffle in his basement.

My uncle called to tell me Grandpa T had died. I was in the middle of infertility treatments, and I had just done an IUI that day. It's another one of those moments that's so clear I remember what I was wearing: a red fleece NBA sweatshirt and very stretchy hormone IUI pants.

I was sitting on the floor between the couch and the coffee table when I got the call, and I remember thinking maybe we created a life as Grandpa was leaving. That thought totally went through my head. I had so hoped that was the case. It wasn't, of course, and I grieved that, as well.

Guardian Angels from Grief

I started Artitudes Design in August of 1995 with a $5,000 loan from my Grandma Gerry. And her utter and total belief in me. My business would not exist today without her.

Grandma Gerry was an amazingly strong woman and a bit of a badass. She was born February 20th, 1920. She had my dad when she was 20 and my uncle when she was 22, and it wasn't long after that her husband left her (for another woman) with two small children. She married again years later, but he died when I was two and she never remarried.

Even though he'll say out loud that he doesn't like women, my dad worshipped my grandmother. As a child, I didn't spend as much time with her as I did with

Grandma T, but we became extremely close when I was a young adult and I even lived with her at one point when I was in my 20s.

Grandma Gerry worked at Boeing; she traveled the world. She came to see me in Denmark in October of 1987, and the next year, she did a huge trip to China. She loved to travel with her friend, Frances, and they did so often.

Grandma Gerry was one of my favorite people in the world. She died the day we got our dog, Lola. We had brought the dog home that day. It was December 20th, 2014. I'll never forget the moment. My phone rang and it was my dad. He said, "Your grandmother has died."

I just folded in on myself, crying with my family right around me and the puppy there. There was such a level grief it was like a dagger to the heart, and I don't usually experience grief that way. For me it's more of a gradual slow burn. But this grief? This was "I can't move" grief.

It was one of those feelings where I knew I'd get out of it. It wasn't that, "Oh my God, I'm going to wallow in this forever," kind of pain. I knew I needed to let go and let it out and be sad, because then I could turn a corner to realize what an amazing life she had and what a priceless influence she'd been on my life.

I am who I am because of both of those ladies, both of those grandmothers. The gift in the grief of their loss was to let myself be sad and let myself feel it. I'm still a work in progress at letting myself feel and move through the emotion.

Grandma Gerry is my guardian angel. She's in the trees when I take a walk. I hear her in my head. She is there looking out for me, calling me on my shit and cheering me on.

Learning from Grief

R ian Fiske was a sweet, kind, amazing soul. He had a presence about him that was humble yet intelligent. He had a way of making people feel seen, and as if he felt what you felt.

Rian worked for me for eight and a half years. He was also my neighbor and my friend. In March 2017, he died from colon cancer, and taught me so much about grief, and myself.

In January 2018, I wrote an article about Rian and published it on LinkedIn. This is what it said:

"Last year was hard. I'd never had an employee die, much less one who was a friend and neighbor as well. Rian's death threw me for a loop, created a tailspin, and sent me into an inertia I hadn't felt before. When you've worked with someone you genuinely admire and respect for nine years, have been neighbors for 11, and have known each other for longer, the cavern created by their loss is deep and echoing. We had a code – we were friends first, then neighbors, and after that he was my employee.

Rian and I didn't agree on everything. He was humble to a fault. It's hard to sell services to clients when you undervalue your own worth daily. He was incredibly religious—in a way that I couldn't relate to. I grew up being told I was a bad person if I didn't do things according to my parent's religious doctrines, so that kind of all-consuming religious ardor is hard for me to digest. But, he was a genuinely good person with a good heart and a quick wit who loved his family deeply.

A year ago today, we had a going away party for Rian. It was a party to celebrate his spirit, his smile, and his zest for life. I thought—I hoped—he'd be back. He wanted so badly to beat the cancer, to fight his way back to health for his family and his life. He gracefully lost that battle in March, just two and a half months after his going away party.

Rian was not my husband, not my brother, not my son. But he was my friend and support and a vital and important part of my days for nearly nine years. We shared a love of stadium 80s rock music. He hated riding in my car with the convertible top down. He made balloon animals and did magic tricks; he drank whiskey and always had a groan-worthy joke ready to tell.

2017 kicked me in the teeth. My eyes don't well up as often now, and I tend to smile at his memory instead. I'm focused on rebuilding what was lost, providing value for our clients, and growing this business into what it's really meant to be.

Losing a friend to cancer is brutal. The only way through it, for me, is chin up, and straight over the mountain to the sunrise. If I learned anything, it's for me not to be so hard on myself, that it's ok to be sad, and that this too shall pass."

I've learned even more since then. I didn't feel like I could grieve Rian. My staff and I wanted to create a video (it's what we do and what Rian did for us) for his memorial service. Rian's family refused our offer.

That was super hard. I felt cheated by that, which I shouldn't have, and I actually think it sounds selfish for me to say that, but we really wanted to give back. We wanted to give back the parts of the Rian that we knew so well and loved. I told Eric, "I feel like I'm not allowed to grieve him because he wasn't mine." And I let myself sit and stew in that space for a very long time.

I eventually made peace with the family's decision not to include us in the service, and I realized he was gone, and it was not for me to control. My memories are mine. Our memories are ours. The family's memories are the family's memories, and they're not going to cross in this case.

Rian died in March and his service was in May. It was a super rainy day. I was still struggling to find a place to put my grief. Now I know there's a term for it. Grief experts call feelings like mine "disenfranchised grief." Defined: Disenfranchised grief is experienced when the death of someone loved is not acknowledged or socially supported.

At Rian's memorial, I saw so many people who knew and loved Rian. One of them, Jeff, was the executive director of a nonprofit we supported, and that Rian had done work for, who came up to me while I was sitting next to Eric. Jeff put his hand on my shoulder and just said, "He knew you loved him." And that was it. Right there I was able to start letting go of that hurt, and knew that it was okay to grieve, in front of my employees and former employees. It was okay.

I'm a better person because of Rian's presence in my life. I'm a better person for the care he took with everyone he met, for the love and care he had for his family, for his religion and his love of God. I'm a better person because I learned from his example.

I was immeasurably impacted by his life and I was devastated by his death. I didn't come out of what I call a depression, kind of downward spiral, until about the November after he died. I was trying to heal, and still had my head in the sand. I didn't want to recognize that he wasn't coming back. As I wrote this I was interviewing for his position. We've not had anyone to truly replace him fully and it's been four years.

Stronger on the Other Side of Grief

I am stronger on the other side of grief. I say that with the understanding that there really may not be another side of grief. Grief is all around us. All the time. It has been my lifelong companion.

I think it's an equalizer for us, collectively. It's also a "name it to tame it" event for me. I'm not trying to put grief aside, but if I don't name the emotion and the feeling, it festers. Naming it recognizes it. I don't move past it because I don't believe we do move past it. It becomes part of our experience, part of who we are and who we will be. My practice with grief is to recognize it and understand it and realize that I can still choose happy. And I can still be sad. The two feelings aren't mutually exclusive.

We didn't conceive a baby when Grandpa died. I mean, it was a sad moment because I had hoped so much that we had. And I have my boys and I'm happy.

Everybody grieves for something, and it's very personal. There are tiny losses. There are huge losses. There are losses all day long for us, for everybody.

We can share the pain of our grief. The world doesn't teach us that, but I've learned the value in sharing the grief in my stories. And I see it equalize us as others share theirs.

Maybe more important is the lesson that the value in grief shows up when we choose what we'll do with it. Some people grieve and believe that the world is out to get them. Some people choose to believe that they are nothing without somebody else who's no longer here. Some people—like me—choose to believe that they are defective if they can't give birth to a baby.

It's okay to feel things. It's not okay to mire yourself in them until they become your identity. It's not okay for me to say I'm defective. It's not okay for me to say there's nowhere else besides my beach house on earth where I can truly be myself. It's not okay for me to *other* myself and stay silent based on someone else's belief system. It's not okay for me to believe my voice doesn't matter.

It's okay to feel sad and it's okay to feel loss, but to live every day as if that loss is a huge hole in my life isn't okay. If I haven't learned from it, it means I'm not growing. I'm not moving. It's means I'm stuck in one place.

I'm not stuck in one place.

As I was writing this chapter, I was on a call with Jeremy, who runs my podcast. He asked, "What are you so happy about?" And I said, "It's a gorgeous, sunny day at the beach! I have a lot of shit swirling and a lot going on. I could choose not to be happy about it, but I am choosing to be happy."

I told him about my brother-in-law who's dying and about my own brother who's in rehab right now, and Jeremy said, "It's always amazing to me the bright attitude you bring to everything."

It's because I choose it. I mean, what is the fucking point of wallowing in self-pity? For me, there's none. There's zero point to it. There are things I'm sad about, but ultimately? Despite all the grief in all of the experiences that have made people say, "Andrea, you should write a book," I believe sharing my grief helps others feel less alone.

You are not alone.

Practice

Your Active Choice

Choose to Gift Your Grief

What if you choose to feel your grief, and share it, give it away to others? What response will that create in you and others? Try it.

Questions

- What is your version of grief?
- Where in your life are you grieving but perhaps not fully aware of it?
- Have you created a victim mindset about any kind of loss? Are you willing to invite your grief to teach you and give you its gifts? (That's a bonus question.)
- What have you gotten from your experience

of grieving that you couldn't have gotten any other way?

Your 10-minute exercise:

Ask a friend to spend 10 minutes sharing their grief with you.

Have extra time? Read a blog post.

https://refugeingrief.com/book/

Final Thoughts

"There is nothing stronger than a woman who has rebuilt herself." – Hannah Gatsby

Don't take yourself too seriously. Laugh a lot. Enjoy the chocolate. Drink the wine. Take the trip. Be silly, by joyful. See the world and be open to other cultures. Realize that life is a lesson every day and learn in each moment. Don't apologize for who you are. Your path is your own and no one else's. You are enough.

Stronger on the Other Side

I think most of the time now, I live on the other side, on the strong side. I don't think I could live there permanently. Well, I could if I were more of an evolved, aware human being. But I'm working on it still. I'm a work in progress.

I live more on the other side now than ever before. I am not weak. I am strong. I am vulnerable. I am thoughtful. I listen, whereas before I knew everything. I know now that when I think I know everything, I'm in a position of weakness, because I'm not open to feedback or input from any other source. And there are so many incredible sources out there who know so much more than I do.

As I said, I never want to be the smartest person in the room. And before I learned that there was an *other* side, a stronger side, I felt like I had to be the smartest, that I always had something to prove. Today I'm more willing to listen than I am to talk.

It is my hope that sharing my shit with you has given you some insight into your own shit. I'd like you to feel like you can do anything and know that even when the world tells you you're a victim of something, that you choose you. I'd like you to know that you and only you are in charge of your own life and the way you respond to your challenges. You respond to the things that are happening, and it's your choice how you do that. Just yours. Only yours.

We Are Enough

In March 2021, as I was completing this book, I decided to write a letter to my younger self to commemorate International Women's Day. It's about me, but it's also about us. I dedicate it to you, wherever you are, whatever you're doing, whatever fires or challenge you're facing. We're all doing the best we can. And we are enough.

Dear Me,

You are enough.

The world will tell you that you're not enough. It will tell you that you can always do better, you should always try harder. It will say in a million ways that you're not the smartest, not the most driven, not the quickest. You'll spend so much time trying to prove yourself and it will be exhausting. You'll see

*things differently when you focus on how amazing you are
rather than looking for where you feel that you're lacking.*

You are enough.

*First, you're going to be okay. You will make it through —
through this, through everything. It won't always seem that
way, but if you choose happiness, if you choose positivity, if
you choose your own path, you'll be okay.*

You are enough.

*Things don't always have to be hard. You do not always have
to prove yourself. No matter how terrible things seem, it
won't be the end of everything. There's always a new day, a
new chapter, the turn of a page.*

You are enough.

*Own your own path. You'll hear so many voices telling you
who you should be, what you should do. But embrace each
moment as your own. Things will change. Change is constant.
Your life will change, your friendships will change, your
circumstances will change. So, live each moment and breathe
each breath. Don't wish away today because the path will wind
away from this moment and onto the next and what seemed to
loom so large will look so small in the rear-view mirror.*

You are enough.

When life throws you down – and it will – consider it a gift to get back up and face down the next challenge. You will turn dark into light. And I promise that, in hindsight, things will be the way they were meant to be. Realize that the only thing within your control is how you choose to react to something. Choose happiness, choose positivity, choose peace.

You are enough.

Don't take yourself too seriously. Laugh a lot. Enjoy the chocolate. Drink the wine. Take the trip. Be silly, by joyful. See the world and be open to other cultures. Realize that life is a lesson every day and learn in each moment.

Don't apologize for who you are. Your path is your own and no one else's.

You are enough.

Hence this book.

Love, Andrea

Acknowledgements

Karen Austin – Thank you for your thoughtful enthusiasm in helping me tell my story in a compelling way. I could not have done this without your care and compassion. It is an honor to call you friend.

Mandy Skey – The gift of your friendship has carried me through my worst times and my best times. When we met 30+ years ago, I had no idea how much your friendship would mean to me throughout my entire life. I am a better person for having you in my life.

Karina Autzen – Du elsker mig lige som jeg er. There is no bigger gift in this world. For your support, your love, and your ability to help me see myself through a different lens – I am forever grateful. Og jeg elsker dig lige som du er.

Carrie Searing – My cheerleader and my reality check. I am so grateful for your presence in my life. I learn from you every day and am honored to call you friend.

Dr. Kristin Kahle – I may never have done this without your support and belief in me. Strong women make the best friends. Thank you!

Kelly & Quinn Zimmerman – The support of your friendship has carried us through rough waters over the years. "There are good ships and there are wood ships, ships that sail the sea, but the best ships are friendships, may they always be." – An Irish Blessing

Kate Race – For executing on my vision and creating beauty in everything you touch. My book cover and graphics tell the story of me. You are amazing.

Lisa Sellge – Copy edits, suggestions, flow. Thank you for reading and rereading and continuing to help me make my story better. You are wonderful.

The Artitudes Team – Carrie, Steve, Laurel, Lisa, Ross, Kate, Grace, Carrie G, John, Heather and Kat. I know I'm the worst client ever so thank you for being accommodating, witty, and gracious. I appreciate the care you all take with our clients and the stunning work we create together.

Beckie & Bruce Hansen – We are so blessed that the fire brought us together. Thank you for your love and support. Family by choice!

Pat Brunstad – For recreating my happy place into something even better than it was before the fire. It's my oasis and truly where I can be my best self. I know what a pain in the ass I was, and I thank you for your grace.

Ryan Ellis – Thank you for a lifetime of support. I'm so glad you are my brother.

Rian Fiske – Even though you are gone, you are not forgotten. You taught me about faith in a higher power and showed your strength of character in everything you did.

Grandma Gerry – My guardian angel. Your belief in me changed my life. I miss you every day.

Eric Heuston – I love you. Even when I don't believe in myself, you always believe in me. This life has been a roller coaster ride, a hike through the wilderness, and a trial by fire. None of it would have been possible without you by my side. I'm forever yours.

Aidan Heuston – My sweet, amazing, kind son. You are a brilliant light that shines so brightly. I am unbelievably humbled that I get to be your mother. I love you forever.

Owen Heuston – The kindest heart, the sweetest soul. Seeing the world through your eyes makes it so much more beautiful. Thank you for your love, it makes me a better person, a better mother. I am honored to be your mom. I love you forever.

Lola – There is no sweeter spirit on earth. Your unwavering devotion makes me want to be a better person if only so that I can become who you believe I already am.

Andrea Heuston is the Founder and CEO of Artitudes Design Inc. and has been in the tech industry for over 30 years. In 2020, she started her own podcast "The Lead Like a Woman Show" focusing on empowering women leaders to empower others through topical discussions and interviews with female leaders. She is passionate about helping to close the gender gap for women in business. Stronger on the Other Side was written to *empower women with the power to choose their own path.* When she's not busy with speaking, writing, hosting, and creative projects, you can find her walking on the beach with her family and two Australian Shepherds.

Made in the USA
Middletown, DE
11 April 2021